797,885 Books
are available to read at

www.ForgottenBooks.com

Forgotten Books' App
Available for mobile, tablet & eReader

ISBN 978-1-330-96455-2
PIBN 10127179

This book is a reproduction of an important historical work. Forgotten Books uses state-of-the-art technology to digitally reconstruct the work, preserving the original format whilst repairing imperfections present in the aged copy. In rare cases, an imperfection in the original, such as a blemish or missing page, may be replicated in our edition. We do, however, repair the vast majority of imperfections successfully; any imperfections that remain are intentionally left to preserve the state of such historical works.

Forgotten Books is a registered trademark of FB &c Ltd.
Copyright © 2017 FB &c Ltd.
FB &c Ltd, Dalton House, 60 Windsor Avenue, London, SW19 2RR.
Company number 08720141. Registered in England and Wales.

For support please visit www.forgottenbooks.com

1 MONTH OF FREE READING

at

www.ForgottenBooks.com

By purchasing this book you are eligible for one month membership to ForgottenBooks.com, giving you unlimited access to our entire collection of over 700,000 titles via our web site and mobile apps.

To claim your free month visit:
www.forgottenbooks.com/free127179

* Offer is valid for 45 days from date of purchase. Terms and conditions apply.

English
Français
Deutsche
Italiano
Español
Português

www.forgottenbooks.com

Mythology Photography **Fiction**
Fishing Christianity **Art** Cooking
Essays Buddhism Freemasonry
Medicine **Biology** Music **Ancient Egypt** Evolution Carpentry Physics
Dance Geology **Mathematics** Fitness
Shakespeare **Folklore** Yoga Marketing
Confidence Immortality Biographies
Poetry **Psychology** Witchcraft
Electronics Chemistry History **Law**
Accounting **Philosophy** Anthropology
Alchemy Drama Quantum Mechanics
Atheism Sexual Health **Ancient History**
Entrepreneurship Languages Sport
Paleontology Needlework Islam
Metaphysics Investment Archaeology
Parenting Statistics Criminology
Motivational

[Almon, John]

BIOGRAPHICAL, LITERARY,

AND

POLITICAL

ANECDOTES,

OF SEVERAL OF

THE MOST EMINENT PERSONS

OF

THE PRESENT AGE.

NEVER BEFORE PRINTED.

WITH AN

APPENDIX;

CONSISTING OF

ORIGINAL, EXPLANATORY, AND SCARCE

PAPERS.

BY THE

AUTHOR OF ANECDOTES OF THE LATE EARL OF CHATHAM.

HISTORIAM, OMNIUM SECRETORUM MEMORIAM DICO.—*Cicero.*

IN THREE VOLUMES.

VOLUME II.

LONDON:

PRINTED FOR T. N. LONGMAN, AND L. B. SEELEY,
IN PATER-NOSTER-ROW.

CONTENTS.

☞ *The References in this Volume to the Appendix, the Reader will find in the Contents of the Appendix.*

CHAPTER XVII.
THE LATE EARL TEMPLE.

Prominent Features of the Opposition to the Earl of Bute. Character of the Opposition. Lesson of the Earl of Bute. Solicits the Friendship of Lord Temple. Contradicts Lord Temple in the House of Lords. Lord George Sackville introduced at Court. Origin of the North Briton. The Opposition formed. Lord Bute makes Proposals to Lord Temple and Mr. Pitt, by Mr. Stanley. The Office of First Minister put into Commission. Desertion of Lord Hardwicke, and others, from the Opposition; whose Offers are rejected by the Court. Lord Temple's Firmness in the Support of Mr. Wilkes, and of the great public Cause. A great Person mistaken in his Opinion of Lord Temple. Opposition re-united. Lord Temple's Advice to Mr. Wilkes. Mr. Webb's Account of Lord Temple. Negotiation concerning the Duke of Leeds. Mr. Pitt's Interview with the King. Lord Holland's Negotiation with the Duke of Bedford. Lord Bute's Mazarinade. Intended Motion on the Seizure of Papers. The Club called the Coterie formed. Opposition divided. Lord Temple's Declaration to the Duke of Newcastle. The Duke of Cumberland's Negotiation with Lord Temple. Terms offered by Lord Temple. Lord Northumberland propofed; rejected. The Duke of Cumberland vifits Mr. Pitt. Remarks. Certainty of Lord Bute's fecret Influence. Lord Temple and Mr. Grenville reconciled. Lord Lyttelton applied to. Lord Holland's Advice to the Duke of Cumberland. Minifters reftored: they difmifs Mr. Stuart Mackenzie, and others. The King fends for Lord Temple and Mr. Pitt. They refufe to accept the Terms offered by the King. The Rockingham Adminiftration formed; they ought to have diffolved the Parliament. Particulars of the Meeting at Lord Eglintoun's. Lord Temple amufed by another Negotiation. Remarks. Duel prevented between Lord Temple and Lord Talbot. Lord Chatham feduced: confeffes in the Houfe of Lords that he had been duped. Lord Temple and Lord Chatham reconciled. Lord Temple refufes the Offer of being made Lord Privy Seal.

Page 1

CHAPTER XVIII.

THE LATE RIGHT HONOURABLE GEORGE GRENVILLE.

Connection with the laft Chapter. Negotiation for Peace. Sir Charles Knowles's Plan for taking the Havannah; prefented to Mr. Grenville, to Lord Temple, to Mr. Pitt, to Lord Anfon, to the Duke of Cumberland. Fortunate Efcape of Admiral Pococke. Mr. Grenville differs with Lord Bute on demanding an Equivalent for the Havannah. Mr. Grenville removed to the Admiralty, and Lord Halifax made Secretary. Mr. Grenville complimented with a Tellerfhip of the Exchequer for his Son. Correfpondence of the Negotiation for Peace fuppofed to be loft. Minifters took their Papers away when removed. Mr.

CONTENTS.

Grenville appointed First Lord of the Treasury. Lawyers not Politicians. Persecution of Mr. Wilkes. Lord Bute's Letter to the King. American Affairs. Project of new-modelling all the American Governments. The Outlines of the Design. True Cause of the Stamp Act. Mr. Grenville not the Author of that Act. Impolicy of it. Mr. Mauduit's Account of a Conference with Mr. Grenville. Remarks on that Paper. Governor Bernard's Letter. Trade and Connection with America explained. Mr. Grenville deceived; removed. Stamp Act repealed. The Plan of subjugating America continued. Montcalm's Letters. Mr. Grenville saves the Public Credit of all Europe. The King's Esteem for Mr. Grenville expressed upon two Occasions. *Page* 65

CHAPTER XIX.
THOMAS WHATELY, ESQ.

His Tracts. Letters to him from Governor Hutchinson and Lieutenant Governor Oliver, shewn to different Persons; sent to America by Dr. Franklin. Resolutions in America upon them. Petition to remove the Governor and Lieutenant Governor. Duel between Mr. Temple and Mr. William Whately. *Page* 103

CHAPTER XX.
CHARLES LLOYD, ESQ.

Names of the Tracts written by him. *Page* 108

CHAPTER XXI.
WILLIAM KNOX, ESQ.

Advocate for the American War. Secretary to Lord George Germain. His State of the Nation; assisted by Mr. Grenville. Other Publications. *Page* 112

CHAPTER XXII.

LORD GEORGE GERMAIN.

Public Prejudice. His Conduct in early Life, and Character. Behaviour at Fontenoy. His Quarrel with Prince Ferdinand. His Conduct at Minden. Observations upon it. Antient Virtue. Modern Indifference. Commencement of the American War. Letter of the late Sir Joseph Yates. Answer to it. Lord George Germain appointed Secretary of State. Management of the London Gazette. Surrender of Lord Cornwallis. Disagreement in the Ministry. The Misfortune of Lord Cornwallis imputed to Lord Sandwich, and to Lord George Germain. This Disagreement appears in Parliament. Conduct of Mr. Dundas and Mr. Rigby. Application to Sir Guy Carleton. Substance of his Letter to the Lord Chancellor. Meeting of the Secret Cabinet. Lord George Germain removed. *Page* 116

CHAPTER XXIII.

DAVID HARTLEY, ESQ.

His Tract intitled " Right of Appeal to Juries, in Causes of Excise, asserted." The Budget. Intended Prosecution of that Tract. His State of the Nation. Letters to his Constituents of Hull. Acquaintance with Dr. Franklin. Appointed Minister Plenipotentiary. His Tract on the French Revolution. *Page* 139

CHAPTER XXIV.

JOSIAH WEDGWOOD, ESQ.

His Discoveries, Taste, and Merits as a Manufacturer; as a Philosopher; as an Inland Navigator. His Instiration of an Association in London, which he called the General Chamber of Manufacturers of Great Britain. His Opposition to Mr. Pitt's Propositions concerning the Trade with Ireland. Account of the Chamber of Manufacturers. The Members of the Chamber differ on the Commercial Treaty with France. The Chamber dissolved. *Page* 164

CHAPTER XXV.

DR. BENJAMIN FRANKLIN.

Founder of American Greatness. Bred at Boston. Printer at Philadelphia. Comes to London. Returns to America. Made Clerk of the Assembly, and Post-master of Philadelphia. Proposes, with Success, an Association to defend the Province. Elected a Member of the General Assembly. Disputes between the Proprietaries and the Assembly. The Answers to the Governor's Messages, ascribed to Dr. Franklin. Quotation from one of them. Made Post-Master-General of all America. Proposes the Congress held at Albany. Plan of the Albany Union. Another Plan proposed, and communicated to Dr. Franklin. His Answers to it. Northern Frontier attacked: levies Troops, and goes to protect it. Sent Agent to England. Settles the Disputes between the Proprietaries and the Assembly. Honours conferred on him in Great Britain. Answers a Pamphlet written by Messieurs Burkes. Returns to America. Receives the Thanks of the Assembly, and rewarded for his Services. Appointed Agent again. His Conduct on this Occasion well known. Visits the Continent of Europe. Petitions, with others, for a Grant of Lands on the Ohio. Report of the Board of Trade againſt the Petition. Dr. Franklin's Anſwer to the Report of the Board of Trade. Prayer of the Petition granted. Lord Hillſborough reſigns on that Account. Affair of Hutchinſon's and Oliver's Letters. Dr. Franklin leaves England. War with America. Appointed Miniſter Plenipotentiary to France. His Conductors removed from the Queen's Houſe. Orrery deſtroyed in America. War ſhould not be made on the Sciences. Several Attempts to open a Negotiation with him at Paris. His Friendſhip for Mr. Silas Deane. Sends Mr. Thornton to England. Inſtance of Mr. Fox's great political Sagacity. Dr. Franklin concludes the Peace between Great Britain and America. He returns to America. His Philoſophy. Dies. Honours to his Memory. *Page* 175

CHAPTER XXVI.

MESSIEURS BURKES.

Four of them. All Literary Men. Fugitive Papers. Series of Letters ſigned Valens. Anſwer to Lord Bath's Pamphlet. Anſwer to Dr. Franklin's Pamphlet. Importance of Guadaloupe. Lord Chatham of Mr. Burke's Opinion, but over-ruled. Value and Importance of the Weſt-Indies. African Trade. Petition and Reſolutions of the Yorkſhire Committee. Mr. Burke's Letter on the Subject of them to the Buckinghamſhire Committee. Several Particulars. *Page* 345

BIOGRA-

BIOGRAPHICAL, LITERARY,
AND
POLITICAL ANECDOTES.

CHAPTER XVII.

THE LATE EARL TEMPLE.

PROMINENT FEATURES OF THE OPPOSITION TO THE EARL OF BUTE.

Character of the Opposition. Lesson of the Earl of Bute. Solicits the Friendship of Lord Temple. Contradicts Lord Temple in the House of Lords. Lord George Sackville introduced at Court. Origin of the North Briton. The Opposition formed. Lord Bute makes Proposals to Lord Temple and Mr. Pitt, by Mr. Stanley. The Office of First Minister put into Commission. Desertion of Lord Hardwicke, and others, from the Opposition; whose Offers are rejected by the Court. Lord Temple's Firmness in the Support of Mr. Wilkes, and of the great public Cause. A Great Person mistaken in his Opinion of Lord Temple. Opposition re-united. Lord Temple's Advice

Advice to Mr. Wilkes. Mr. Webb's Account of Lord Temple. Negotiation concerning the Duke of Leeds. Mr. Pitt's Interview with the King. Lord Holland's Negotiation with the Duke of Bedford. Lord Bute's Mazarinade. Intended Motion on the Seizure of Papers. The Club called the Coterie formed. Opposition divided. Lord Temple's Declaration to the Duke of Newcastle. The Duke of Cumberland's Negotiation with Lord Temple. Terms offered by Lord Temple. Lord Northumberland proposed; rejected. The Duke of Cumberland visits Mr. Pitt. Remarks. Certainty of Lord Bute's secret Influence. Lord Temple and Mr. Grenville reconciled. Lord Lyttelton applied to. Lord Holland's Advice to the Duke of Cumberland. Ministers restored: they dismiss Mr. Stuart Mackenzie, and others. The King sends for Lord Temple and Mr. Pitt. They refuse to accept the Terms offered by the King. The Rockingham Administration formed: they ought to have dissolved the Parliament. Particulars of the Meeting at Lord Eglintoun's. Lord Temple amused by another Negotiation. Remarks. Duel prevented between Lord Temple and Lord

Lord Talbot. Lord Chatham seduced: confesses in the House of Lords that he had been duped. Lord Temple and Lord Chatham reconciled. Lord Temple refuses the Offer of being made Lord Privy Seal.

THE vigorous opposition that was made to the measures of the Earl of Bute, during that noble Lord's administration, and some years afterwards, was considerably animated by the spirit and zeal of Lord Temple. So true it is, that in all great points of public interest, where the union of individuals is necessary, there must be, if not a leader, at least a person of weight sufficient, not only to form the union, but to give energy to its measures. In this instance, Lord Temple was that person. Perhaps it would be strictly correct, to style him the leader of the opposition.

The persons who composed this opposition were of the first rank, family, and fortune in the kingdom. They were zealously attached to the constitution, as it was established at the revolution, and to the family on the throne.

throne. There has not been, since the accession of the house of Hanover, an opposition to ministerial tyranny formed upon purer principles of public happiness and interest. All former oppositions were tinctured with Jacobitism. This was the first against whom that charge could not be brought; and the phænomenon is increased, when it is observed, that the notorious friends of the house of Stuart, and the descendants of those, who, in their day, had been the notorious friends of the same house, and who avowedly professed all the slavish principles and doctrines of the Stuarts, now publicly filled the court of the King, and several of the principal departments in the state. The Earl of Bute was omnipotent. He not only dismissed the great ministers, who had conducted the war with unexampled vigour and success, but he turned out every friend of the house of Hanover, who held any office or place under the crown. These circumstances were sufficient to suspect a design in the prime minister to renew the measures of the second Charles and James. His conduct created hatred, and his principles produced alarm.

At

At this time was inculcated that unhappy lesson, "That the more unpopular a King's minister becomes, the more firmly he ought to be supported——Kings must never recede." If ever there was a time, when this doctrine was more pernicious in its effects than at another, it was at this time. Ample experience has convinced every person, of the losses, disgraces, and miseries, which are to be ascribed to this source.

The principal, and almost only fact, urged in his behalf, was, that he was the *Favourite* of the King. Those who made this apology were exceedingly indiscreet. *Royal favourites* have always been odious in all countries. Their invariable design constantly is, to reduce the people to a state of insignificancy, in order that they may establish their own power with impunity.

A few weeks after he had driven Lord Temple and Mr. Pitt from their offices, he made a pointed and personal attack upon Lord Temple, in the House of Lords, before any system or plan of opposition to him had been formed, or probably even thought of; for they refigned in the month of October 1761, and this attack was made in the fucceeding month of November, which was a confiderable time before the general difmiffion and profcription of the Whigs took place. Lord Bute fought the firft opportunity to make it. He faw in Lord Temple, that rifing fpirit he might have moft caufe to dread. He had folicited conciliation with his Lordfhip about ten days before, and had failed. Warmed with refentment, and flattered with the hope of obtaining a triumph over his opponent,—upon the motion for the papers relative to the rupture with Spain, Lord Temple, after recommending unanimity in the ftrongeft terms, begged to make but one obfervation upon all that had been faid concerning the family compact, which was, that it had been figned in Auguft, had been ratified in September, and the written advice to his Majefty was given and dated on the eighteenth of that month. Upon which, Lord Bute rofe in great heat, and gave to Lord Temple the moft flat and unqualified contradiction. He declared upon *his honour*, that there was *no* intelligence

telligence of such a fact so constituted, at that time. These words brought up Lord Temple again; who likewise declared upon *his honour*, that there *was* intelligence of the highest moment relative to those matters at that time; that he was not at liberty to declare it publicly, but would *refresh* his Lordship's memory in private: and then beckoned Lord Bute to follow him out of the house; who did: and in the private conference between them, Lord Bute admitted that he recollected the facts, as they had been stated; but when he returned into the House of Lords, he did not, which, as a gentleman, he ought to have done, stand up in his place, and acknowledge his mistake. The reader will not think it improbable, that Lord Temple's enmity to Lord Bute was embittered by this circumstance. Nor will it perhaps be improper to take notice of another circumstance, which was indeed of lesser moment, but not less personally insulting to the feelings of Lord Temple and Mr. Pitt. On the first court-day, after the accession of the present King, and while the late King lay dead in his palace, Lord George Sackville made his appearance at St James's, and was admitted to kifs the King's hand. This was such an outrage on the memory of the late King, and on the honour of those servants who had the conduct of the war, that they were perfectly astonished at it, and made inquiry into the cause of it; when, to their no less surprise, they found that Lord George had been invited to court by the Earl of Bute. They remonstrated strongly against it; and Lord George did not appear again at St. James's during Mr. Pitt's administration.

In the month of May 1762, Lord Bute having advanced himself to the head of the Treasury, and dismissed many of the principal Whigs from their offices, the great families were convinced of the dangerous designs of the Favourite, and embraced the recommendations of Lord Temple, to unite, and to form a powerful opposition to his measures and conduct. In order to prevent this union becoming established, to an extent that might be fatal to his influence, he opened all the floodgates of corruption. Sixteen peerages were created; the Lords of the Bedchamber were doubled; the Grooms of the Bedchamber were

were doubled; the salaries of other places were doubled; obsolete places were revived; many were pensioned out of offices, to make vacancies for others. In a word, the whole power and patronage of the crown were exerted to the utmost to support his administration. This dominion, great and absolute as it was, did not content him. He was conscious, that though the power of the crown was amply sufficient to give him all that he wanted in parliament, he saw there was something else wanting. This was the favour of the people. And in order to obtain this, he hired a considerable number of writers; Smollett, Murphy, Mallett, Shebbeare, Ruffhead, Cleland, Guthrie, and many more. On the day that he mounted the Treasury steps, a paper called *the Briton* made its appearance in his favour, written by Smollett; and in a few days followed another, called *the Auditor*, and several more. In these papers, the characters of Mr. Pitt and Lord Temple were repeatedly reviled, in terms the most opprobrious and scurrilous. And though it was not probable, that such writings could have much effect on the public mind, yet it must have

have been observed by those persons who have given some attention to this literary species of belligerent operation, that an impression may be made by numerous and constant efforts. Add to this, the writers in behalf of the ministry have always a great advantage over their opponents; they can indulge in asserting the most infamous falsehoods, with impunity.

To counteract the poison of these papers, a gentleman of talents and erudition, who was a warm and sincere admirer of Lord Temple's patriotism and virtues, commenced another paper; which was called *the North Briton*. The elegance of the composition, the keenness of the satire, and the brilliancy of the wit, with which almost every paper abounded, very soon attracted the public attention; and secured to the paper a very extensive circulation. Lord Temple was not ignorant of his friend's design, before he put it in execution; and certainly approved of it. But the severity of some of the national reflections upon the Scots, on account of their attachment to Lord Bute, and their enmity

to

to Mr. Pitt, did not meet with the entire approbation of his Lordship; not from any personal considerations of his own, but from an apprehension of thereby weakening the national force. However, it must always be remembered, that in the language of a temporary periodical paper, the bent and humour of the times must be considered; and to give such a paper popularity and consequence, sacrifices must be made to the caprice of the day. At this time, a great part of the Scots were exceedingly illiberal to the English; and a great part of the English were no less offended with the Scots. Lord Bute was undoubtedly, by his partiality to his countrymen, the primary cause of these jealousies.

Lord Temple frequently assisted his friend in the production of these papers; not indeed with his pen, but with his information and line of reasoning. All the Whigs highly approved of these papers: the public mind was strongly impressed by them: the language and argument were always judicious, and directed to the objects of the moment: while the papers of **Lord Bute's** writers, were clumsily

sily put together; were disgusting by their scurrility, and contemptible by their dulness.

This literary assistance from Lord Temple and his friends, gave additional weight to his Lordship's recommendation of a union; and the measure was completely accomplished in the month of February 1763.

To give a signal to the nation of this union, to contradict the assertions of the ministerial writers that the persons in opposition were totally unconnected, and to inspire the public mind with the hope of relief, from the all-grasping power and insolent domination of a Favourite; the principals agreed to dine together, once a week, at each other's houses. The first dinner was at Lord Temple's in Pall-Mall, about the end of February 1763; the next was at the Duke of Newcastle's, in March following; others succeeded. The parties were chiefly the Dukes of Bolton, Devon, Grafton, Newcastle, Portland; Marquis of Rockingham; Earls of Albemarle, Ashburnham, Besborough, Cornwallis, Hardwicke, Scarborough, Spencer, Temple; Lords Abergavenny, Dacre, Fortescue, rescue, Grantham, Sondes, Walpole, Villiers; Right Hon. W. Pitt, Sir George Savile, C. Townshend, C. Yorke, James Grenville, &c. &c. This flag, as it was called at the time, for the names were constantly given every week in the newspapers, was a testimonial to the whole country, that there was an opposition formed, composed of many of the first personages in the kingdom. The Favourite was their object. To correct the mischiefs he had committed, and to prevent the continuance of his power, were their avowed designs. After the second meeting of the party, when he saw the measure likely to be pursued, he was seized with timidity: he caused an offer to be made to Lord Temple and Mr. Pitt, by Mr. Hans Stanley, that if they would withdraw from the Whigs, he would make an opening for them to return to administration. They treated the proposal with the utmost indignation; they considered it an insult offered to their integrity; and refused it with a firmness that was worthy of imitation. They had made their engagements, they said, and were incapable of breaking them.

This

This attempt to divide his opponents indisputably shews, that he was afraid of their united strength, and that whatever other reasons he might have, he was, from this moment, entertaining thoughts of retiring from before the curtain. He was by this time, also, become afraid of other adversaries; who were his coadjutors in the negotiation of peace. They had been duped, and began to threaten him. Therefore, thus finding his offers rejected by his *public* opponents, he made offers to his *private* enemies; by whom they were accepted. This was the true cause of that sudden succession of Mr. Grenville, and the Lords Halifax and Egremont, to the unprecedented copartnership of premier; for when Lord Bute resigned in April 1763, it was immediately signified to all the foreign ministers, by authority, " That his Majesty had been pleased to place his government in the hands of Mr. Grenville, the Earls of Halifax and Egremont; and that in all cases of importance, they were not to act separately, but in an agreement of the *three:* And to them all applications on business were to be directed." This is the first time that the
office

office of prime minister was put into commission. Lord Bute, in the most solemn manner, assured his successors, that he renounced all pretensions to public business in every shape whatever.

During the arrangement of this change of ostensible ministers, the weekly publication of the North Briton was suspended, from April 2 to April 23. When the new ministry were declared by authority, the writer of that paper attacked them with great asperity; and in the same paper animadverted on the King's speech, which had been delivered a few days before at the close of the session of Parliament. These animadversions provoked the court exceedingly; and it was instantly resolved to take advantage of this pretended insult on the King, and under colour of that pretence, to exercise the extremest vengeance on all parties concerned in the North Briton. Lord Bute urged his substitutes to do what he durst not attempt himself: he was smarting under the wounds inflicted by former papers. He therefore eagerly seized this first moment to gratify his desire of revenge. The crown lawyers seconded

seconded his wishes. Prerogative lawyers are always ready to denominate any political paper a libel. But the better opinion is that this was a constitutional paper: the King was treated with the greatest personal respect, his ministers only were condemned.

A little time afterwards, Lord Temple wrote, or, perhaps it will be correctly stating, that his Lordship dictated to an amanuensis, a fair and constitutional defence of this paper of the North Briton. A few copies only o this defence were printed; it was not published. The following extracts are taken from one of the copies:

" Every one does not know exactly the principles of the constitution, by which we are to judge with what degree of authority a speech from the throne is stamped, whether it is to be considered as personal to the King, or ascribed to the ministers; and how far it is sacred above any other act of administration whatever, and exempt from the freedom of discussion with which all ministerial transactions may be treated. The rights of Majesty

jesty are venerable · and no good subject

respect that is due to the Sovereign. It was therefore very artful to raise a cry against the alleged author of the *North Briton*, that he had affronted the King, and to proclaim aloud, that whoever countenanced him, or avowed what he advanced, was a partaker of his offence. Perhaps some were stunned with this at first: duty to his Majesty might be too strong for the rights of liberty, and fear of being disrespectful to the King might silence the claims of truth. But when people recovered from the first surprise, and examined the affair coolly, it was impossible not to see through the ministerial artifice. There are of those, who will have no superiors in loyalty, and cannot be exceeded by any in personal respect, duty, and affection to the King, and yet will not easily yield the freedom of examining what ministers are pleased to put into the speeches they make for the throne. Nor will they join in a cry against any man, were he ever so culpable in other respects, as affronting the King, for doing what they think is the privilege of every subject to do.

That is wounding the conftitution, under pretence of regard to royalty. The refpect due to his Majefty, in that matter, is to diftinguifh him from the Minifters; to exculpate the King, as the conftitution does, from any wrong; and to lay the fault, if there is one, upon the Minifters, whofe, moft indifputably, it is.

" It is a queftion of too much magnitude to be confounded with any thing elfe, what liberty the conftitution allows to be taken with the King's fpeech; and therefore it ought to be confidered by itfelf: but the ftrongeft prejudices cannot carry any man, who will ufe his own eyes and underftanding, to believe that the author of the *North Briton*, number forty-five, meant an infult to the King. All he has faid, is levelled againft the minifters, and he exprefles, in a variety of fentences, the utmoft refpect for his Sovereign; a heart-felt duty and affection to his perfon; a high veneration for his qualities; and an undiffembled attachment to his royal houfe, and the fucceffion to the crown in the Proteftant line.

" The

" The author has waged perpetual war with Toryism and disaffection. Nothing has been more complained of in the whole course of the paper, than that, ever since the *Favourite*'s influence became predominant, the staunch, known, and tried friends of this royal family, have been depressed; and the avowed enemies of it unreasonably elevated. It is not reasonable to think that such a writer should mean to give a personal affront to the King. But nothing can be further from every expression in the paper, about which so much noise has been made. It is impossible to torture it into an insult to Majesty, unless the word *Minister* is the same with the word *King*; and unless the strongest expressions of regard for the Prince upon the throne are not only to have no meaning at all allowed them, but are even to be interpreted into invectives against the Sovereign, whose applause they found.

" The paper begins with laying this foundation, that ' the King's speech has always ' been considered by the legislature, and by ' the public at large, as *the speech of the Minis-* ' *ter.*'

'*ter.*' The speech, there treated of, is called an instance of *ministerial effrontery*. It is expressly named in every part of the paper, the *Minister's speech*. The author signifies his 'doubt, whether the *imposition* he complains 'of, is greater *on the Sovereign*, or on the Na- 'tion.' The lamentation he makes, is 'that 'a *Prince of the excellent character he describes*, 'can be *brought* to give the sanction of his 'sacred name to unjustifiable public declara- 'tions from a throne, renowned for truth, 'honour, and unsullied virtue.'

" It is *the Minister*, who, it is said, is held in contempt and abhorrence for it. *He*, it is said, *has made our Sovereign declare* that in which lies the *fallacy* inveighed against: it is called a strain of insolence in the *Minister*, to lay claim to what he is conscious all his efforts tended to prevent. After asserting that no hireling of the Minister had been hardy enough to dispute what he had advanced, it is said, ' Yet *the Minister* himself *has made* ' *our Sovereign declare*,' &c.—' The *Minister*'s ' *speech* (it is said) dwells on the approbation ' given by Parliament to the Preliminary Arti- ' cles.'

'cles.'—' *The Minister* cannot forbear, even 'in the King's speech, insulting us with a dull ' repetition of the word œconomy,' and ' in ' vain will such *a Minister* preach up in the ' speech that spirit of concord,' &c. In short, it is the *Minister*, and nothing but the Minister, which runs through the whole paper; and all the wrong complained of is charged upon the *Minister*.

" A political paper wrote a great many years ago, to expose the danger of making writings criminal by *inuendoes*, proved a treatise on the small-pox to be the blackest treason, by translating the word *variol* to mean *government*, and adapting every other term according to the same dictionary. Sure no other method can succeed in proving that there is an insult aimed at the King in this paper.

" It is a different affair, whether the author of the *North Briton* is right or wrong, in what he has advanced in the several places of the paper, where he uniformly pursues the above dialect; or whether the fundamental principle, on which he proceeds, be a just one or no. But, is he arraigning the *Minister*, or insulting *Majesty?*—Is it the *King*, or the *Minister*, that he charges with what he alleges is wrong? Can any man lay his hand on his heart and say, that the person who wrote that paper, has said the *King* is the author of a fallacy; because he has charged the *Minister* with having imposed on the Sovereign, and, by imposition, made him declare a thing which is a fallacy? We may confound *Majesty* and *Ministers* as we please, when we wish to destroy the distinction, for the purpose of making *royal veracity* a protection to *ministerial fallacy*; but this writer separates them with the plainest discrimination—He gives to each his part—The one, he says, is *imposed upon*; the other is *the author of the imposition*. Which of these is the crime? Any person may be imposed upon, but he is innocent; none can impose upon another without being criminal. Royalty does not deify human nature; and what man, or what King, so wise and so able, as not, in some instance or other, to have been imposed upon? It is the common lot of humanity to be liable to deception: but that sort of imposition that

springs

springs from misinformation, or want of just information, it is not in the power of any man to secure himself against; and, of all others, Kings are most liable to it.

" The author of the *North Briton*, number *forty-five*, is not contented with the most explicit language that the English tongue affords, to point out, beyond a possibility of being mistaken, that it is the *Minister* he accuses; and that, so far from charging *Majesty*, the very charge itself is, having *imposed upon the King*—Not contented with this, he gives the King's character, in terms full of respect, as a *Prince of so many great and amiable qualities, whom England truly reveres.*—This is not the language of insult.

" The regard he expresses in this very paper for the late good King, is an irresistible proof of the affection and attachment of the person who wrote it, to his present Majesty, and all the royal family.—Part of his indignation against the *Minister*, is for not shewing a due regard to the honour, either of our late gracious Sovereign, or of his present Majesty.

' Was it (fays he) a *tender regard* for the ho-
' nour of the late King, or of his prefent Ma-
' jefty, that invited to court Lord George Sack-
' ville?' Nobody is at a lofs to know what branch of the royal family he defcribes, as *the moft amiable Princefs in the world*, who, it is fuppofed, is to make happy a diftinguifhed Prince of the fame illuftrious line. Is that the ftyle of the enemies of his Majefty's family? How does he fpeak of the *fecurity of the houfe of Hanover?* ' What a fhame (fays
' he) was it to fee the fecurity of this country,
' in point of military force, complimented
' away, *contrary to the opinion of royalty itfelf*,
' and facrificed to the prejudices, and to the
' ignorance of a fet of people, the moft unfit,
' from every confideration, to be confulted on
' a matter relative to the fecurity of *the houfe*
' *of Hanover.*' He fpeaks, with high fatisfaction, *of a loyal and affectionate people*; an idea that could give no pleafure to a perfon difaffected to his Majefty's auguft family, or inclined to affront the King. No man, that is not a hearty friend to his Majefty, and to the Proteftant fucceffion of the crown in his family, would write in fuch a ftrain. The
words

words are ftronger than a thoufand arguments. Such things do not look like a defign to alienate the affections of his Majefty's fubjects, or ftir up traitorous infurrections againft his government. *That* belongs to thofe who have no good-will to the houfe of Hanover; whofe loyalty is attached to an exiled and abjured family. When the author of the *North Briton* fpeaks of that family, (as he does in this paper,) he ufes another kind of tone. ' The *Stuart line* (fays he) has ever
' been intoxicated with the flavifh doctrines of
' the abfolute, independent, unlimited power
' of the crown."

The feveral particulars of the profecutions of the printers, publifhers, and fuppofed author, with all the other circumftances concerning them, have been fo fully and repeatedly given to the public, it is not neceffary to fay any thing of them here; except only fuch matters as have been either miftated or omitted in the former accounts.

The firft, and moft material of thefe, is the conduct of fome individuals in the body of
the

the Whigs; whom Lord Temple had taken such pains to unite. These individuals were headed by the Earl of Hardwicke. As soon as Mr. Wilkes had been discharged by the Court of Common Pleas, they immediately paid their devoirs at St. James's, to shew to the court they disapproved of Mr. Wilkes, of his friends, and of his cause. This scandalous desertion was treated, even by the court, as it deserved. They were not the persons whom Lord Bute wanted. Finding this offered treachery not sufficient for their purpose, they entered into a league to uphold and defend general warrants; and because Mr. Wilkes had been discharged upon his privilege, as a member of parliament, it was another condition of the leaguers, in order to cast an odium on the Chief Justice of the Commons Pleas, to vote away privilege of parliament in the case of a libel. This latter fact was not known, until that vote had passed. The Duke of Newcastle mentioned it at a meeting of the party at Devonshire-house, which meeting was held for the purpose of settling the words of a protest against that vote. This protest was principally

pally written by Lord Temple. And when they came to the confideration of figning it, the Duke of Newcaftle excufed himfelf, on account of his friend Lord Hardwicke: and then explained the nature and extent of their engagement.

Lord Temple's fpirit and firmnefs in fupport of the caufe of Mr. Wilkes, whofe caufe was that of every man who had any regard for conftitutional liberty, deferved, and met with, the higheft applaufe from every part of England. It was his purfe which carried on the feveral law-fuits againft the King's meffengers, and others. It was his liberality, munificence, and activity, which decided this great caufe, in favour of the public. The caufe muft have funk under the weight of minifterial influence and oppreffion, if it had not been fupported by his intrepidity and perfeverance. In this he was alone—even Mr. Pitt thought his fpirit was too high. But if it was a fault—it was a virtuous fault—it was a fault in behalf of the people;—whofe caufe, upon all occafions, he dearly loved and cherifhed. When Mr. Wilkes was committed, his Lordfhip offered to bail him in any sum; if one hundred thousand pounds were required, he declared his recognizance was ready.

This public espousal of Mr. Wilkes, brought upon his Lordship the most distinguished marks of ministerial insult and malice; yet such was his complacency to the necessary dignity of government, that he permitted the first Lord of the Treasury to be re-elected for the town of Buckingham, rather than suffer the King's first Minister to mendicate a seat in parliament. His mind was influenced by public considerations, not by personal ones. Few men's characters have been more mistaken, or more misrepresented, than his Lordship's. When a Great Personage said of him, " That he was undoubtedly a great man, but that he loved to embarrass government," he only shewed that he had been misinformed. No man could be more zealously attached to a constitutional government than he was. But he detested, with fervency and sincerity, a government of secrecy, hypocrisy, and treachery.

This

This conduct of Lord Temple restored unanimity to the opposition, except Lord Hardwicke, and two or three more; and opposition became cordially united, in the general wish of bringing all the late proceedings before parliament.

Mr. Wilkes employed the space of time between his enlargement from the Tower, and the meeting of parliament, in printing the North Britons in his house. This circumstance gave Lord Temple much concern: he begged Mr. Wilkes to lay aside the design; and when he had begun to put it in execution, his Lordship implored him to desist. Mr. Wilkes, however, would not; he said many of his friends in the city had desired to subscribe for a neat and correct edition of the North Briton. It should here be stated, that the ground of Lord Temple's objection to Mr. Wilkes re-printing the North Briton in his house, was this, that amongst all the printers and booksellers, whom the ministry had attached on account of the North Briton, there was not to be found a tittle of evidence that could reach Mr. Wilkes; "Consequently," said Lord Temple to Mr. Wilkes, "you

"you ought not to furnish your enemies now with the means of obtaining that evidence which you have hitherto had prudence to prevent: and as to the plan of subscription, he added, particularly, that Mr. Wilkes could not name the extent of the sum of money he was ready to advance, if Mr. Wilkes would but send away his printing-press." Mr. Wilkes was deaf to all entreaties. He printed the North Briton; and the event justified Lord Temple's apprehensions. The ministry bribed one of Mr. Wilkes's journeymen to become evidence against him; he was tried for *re-printing* and *re-publishing* the North Briton; upon that evidence *only* he was convicted: there was no evidence at all against him upon the *original* publication. Had he therefore followed Lord Temple's advice, the victory of public liberty must have been complete; the ministers must have been dismissed; and censured at least, if not impeached. Lord Temple often lamented this unfortunate part of Mr. Wilkes's conduct.

When parliament met, the Bishop of Gloucester (Dr. Warburton) suddenly rose in the House of Lords, and complained of a breach of privilege; his name being printed to a note in an obscene poem, called an *Essay on Woman*; a few copies of which had been printed by Mr. Wilkes, at the press in his own house. The same journeyman who had been bribed to rob and betray him, was the evidence against him in this matter also. This complaint perfectly astonished Lord Temple: he knew nothing of the poem. But when he heard that it came from Mr. Wilkes's private press, he was so sensibly affected, he was obliged to leave the House. Upon the charge of the North Briton, he had prepared to defend that paper, and also the conduct of the Chief Justice, (Pratt,) who had discharged Mr. Wilkes upon his privilege, as a member of parliament. On these two points he had determined to combat the arguments of the ministers and their lawyers.

In the debate on Mr. Wilkes's expulsion in the month of January 1764, Mr. Rigby spoke of Lord Temple's public manner of approving, supporting, and defending the conduct of Mr. Wilkes, in terms of asperity and harshness.

harshness. He was answered with great ability and spirit by Mr. James Grenville; who drew a picture of the Duke of Bedford in such strong colours, that the House was obliged to interfere. Mr. Webb, Solicitor of the Treasury, acknowledged that Lord Temple's conduct had, in one point, been much misrepresented; for amongst Mr. Wilkes's papers seized at his house, he had found a letter from Lord Temple to that gentleman, expressing the strongest disapprobation of the abuse of the Scots in the North Britons.

When the ministers had gone through the first part of the storm concerning Mr. Wilkes, they began to perceive that their late proceedings would be vigorously attacked in parliament; and that they should meet with a powerful opposition there. On this account, they began to consider of filling up some vacancies which had happened, and of strengthening themselves with some alliances. The president's chair had been vacant from the beginning of the year 1763, by the death of Earl Granville: this they proposed filling with the Duke of Leeds; and they consulted Lord

Lord Bute upon it. This very circumftance

doubted fact, clearly fhews that they had no influence in the clofet.

Lord Bute, who had gone to Harrowgate to be out of the way of the ftorm, returned to London upon this bufinefs: he inftantly put his *veto* on the propofition refpecting the Duke of Leeds. Whether he had fome other perfon in contemplation, or whether he began to repent of having made the prefent minifters, and was looking out for another fet to fucceed them, is not certain; but if we may judge from what foon after appeared, the latter feems to have been the cafe. This difagreement between the miniftry and Lord Bute was not fettled when Lord Egremont died at the beginning of Auguft 1763: this unexpected event brought the difpute to a crifis. There being now two feats in the cabinet vacant, which in the fmall number of five, for the cabinet at that time confifted of no more, was nearly equal to a fufpenfion of public bufinefs; a fituation that could not laft long.

Lord Bute was still desirous of gaining Lord Temple and Mr. Pitt; but as Lord Temple had refused his applications twice before, the first time early in the month of November 1761, and the other in the month of March 1763, he resolved to make this third application to Mr. Pitt. And having found Mr. Pitt more civil than Lord Temple had been, he brought Mr. Pitt to the King, for the purpose of forming a new administration. But Mr. Pitt having stated to his Majesty in the way of explanation, his inviolable union with the great Whig families, and in effect, what had been given, in the way of answer, to Mr. Stanley in March last, Lord Bute took fright, and broke off the negotiation entirely. Lord Bute's view in this business did not extend beyond a partial change: he wished to bring in Lord Temple and Mr. Pitt, and two or three others, but not more; and to continue to hold the reins of government by his secret influence: and when he had made them odious and insignificant, as he did every body else, he could turn them out at pleasure, without offending the nation. They knew all this: and he knew, that Lord Temple and

and Mr. Pitt, with the great body of the Whigs, would form an administration of such power and strength, that his influence would be totally annihilated. To his vanity, and lust of power, was sacrificed this opportunity of forming a strong and popular government. The particulars of the conference between his Majesty and Mr. Pitt have been already printed in the Anecdotes of Mr. Pitt, chap. xxv.

The Favourite's next resource was to Lord Holland for advice in his present critical situation; for by his last manœuvre he had made both parties his enemies. Lord Holland advised him to continue the present ministers in their places, and to fill up the vacancies with the Duke of Bedford and Lord Sandwich. But as this was a negotiation in which Lord Bute could not appear, Lord Holland undertook it for him, and managed the matter very adroitly; by which he blunted the Duke of Bedford's enmity to Lord Bute, on account of the late peace; and the ministers were allowed to make a sort of proscription of Lord Bute on account of the late indignity he had shewn them, in offering to displace them for Mr. Pitt and Lord Temple; and to compensate the Duke of Leeds, they were permitted to offer him an adequate pension, which his Grace accepted. The Duke of Bedford insisted upon Lord Holland promising, in the name of Lord Bute, (for which he had Lord Bute's authority,) that his Lordship would not in future interfere, intrigue, or disturb the present ministers, in any department of their offices, in any of their recommendations to the King, or in any of the measures of government.

When the arrangements were all made, Lord Bute retired to his estate in Bedfordshire; and the ministers boasted that they had exiled him: Lord Temple called it a *Mazarinade*; alluding to a similar conduct of Cardinal Mazarine, who governed France as absolutely when absent from court as when in it.

The question respecting general warrants, which was brought forward in the succeeding session of parliament, is well known; but there was another question, which Lord Temple

ple was very anxious to have had brought on; this was concerning the feizure of papers. He was not lefs defirous of obtaining a ftrong condemnation of this practice, than he was of the condemnation of general warrants. But Mr. Charles Yorke firft, and after him feveral others of the minority, declared their entire difapprobation of the intended motion, fo it was never brought forward. It is impoffible to account for their objections; Lord Temple was fomewhat chagrined by the refufal: and he wrote a tract upon the fubject, or at leaft dictated the greateft part of it, intitled, " A Letter to the Secretaries of State, on the Seizure of Papers." The reader will find an extract from it in the Appendix, marked H.

Many of the gentlemen who compofed the oppofition, or minority as they were at this time more frequently called, faw with concern and pain thefe occafional divifions : and to prevent, if poffible, the mifchiefs arifing from them, they agreed to inftitute a club, or fociety, confifting of the minority. They were called the *Coterie;* and met at a houfe in Albemarle-ftreet. The object of the inftitution ſtitution was ſingly *to preſerve union:* but after ſubſiſting about five or ſix months, the number of members began to diminiſh, the meetings were ſeldom, and at length the project was abandoned. At the commencement of this inſtitution there was a quarto pamphlet publiſhed, called, "A Letter from Albermarle-ſtreet to the Cocoa Tree, on ſome late Tranſ-actions," which, though not literally written by Lord Temple, was entirely written under his eye, and nearly every line dictated by him. One deſign of it was, to proclaim the creed, or what he hoped was and would continue to be the creed of the minority, from the head-quarters; that the nation might know the doctrines they profeſſed, and the principles they avowed. But though the pamphlet was generally approved by the nation, yet there were ſome perſons in the minority who thought it declared too much. The reader will find ſome extracts from it in the Appendix, marked I.

This was the laſt effort Lord Temple made to preſerve unanimity among the noblemen and gentlemen who had formed themſelves into an oppoſition, in the hope, as they ſaid, of rescuing the government of the country from the influence of the royal Favourite. When the club in Albemarle-street ceased, the minority, as a party, nearly ceased also. The leader was discomfited; he was in earnest against Lord Bute; but many of the others were not: they were ready to enlist under his banners whenever he was disposed to receive them. Mr. Charles Yorke accepted of a patent of precedence, which shewed his readiness to enter into the ministerial service. At length this schism came to an explanation between Lord Temple and the Duke of Newcastle. Lord Temple, in the plainest terms, assured his Grace, that if the only object of opposition was the possession of *places*, if nothing was intended for the public, if his Grace and his friends would neither propose nor support any measure for the security of the liberties of the people, he would continue no longer a cover to that design. With this declaration the opposition, or minority, totally ceased as a body.

During the succeeding session of parliament, which commenced in the month of January 1765.

1765, Mr. Pitt did not attend. Upon the Regency bill, which was brought in towards the end of the session, the minority consisted of only thirty-seven members. The ministers now thought themselves perfectly secure; and having submitted in several instances to Lord Bute's interfering in the patronage of their departments, the minority being broken and dispersed, they began to assume an independence of spirit and character; they remonstrated strongly against Lord Bute's conduct, against his breach of promise, against his secret advice of measures; they complained of being kept in total ignorance of those measures, (the Regency bill, &c.) until called upon to carry them into execution; of recommendations of persons to high and lucrative situations without their participation or even knowledge; and lastly, of the King's confidence not being placed in the constitutional channels.

This conduct of theirs determined their fate: it was resolved to remove them. Lord Bute applied to the Duke of Cumberland; no doubt with his Majesty's knowledge and approbation. His Royal Highness sent for Lord

Lord Temple on the 15th of May 1765. It will occur to the reader's obfervation, that notwithftanding the unfortunate ftate of the late minority, Lord Temple ftill continued to be the *firft* perfon the court were defirous of obtaining. In the conference which followed between his Royal Highnefs and his Lordfhip, the Duke informed Lord Temple, that his Majefty was refolved to change his fervants; and wifhed to engage his Lordfhip, Mr. Pitt, and their friends; and then very gracioufly condefcending to acknowledge his Lordfhip's public virtues, and public fpirit, his Royal Highnefs requefted to be informed of the terms which his Lordfhip had in contemplation to propofe, previous to his undertaking the adminiftration. Lord Temple, with the greateft decency and humility, folicited to reprefent to his Royal Highnefs,

Firft, concerning continental affairs, the making of certain foreign alliances:

And a removal of fome mifunderftandings in thofe already made.

Secondly,

Secondly, concerning domestic affairs; his Lordship required the restoration of officers, civil as well as military, who had been barbarously dismissed from their places and situations without cause, or charge of crime. A complete condemnation of general warrants: and his Lordship added with a strong emphasis, a full condemnation of the seizure of papers, except in a charge, upon oath, of high treason.

His Royal Highness paused a moment, and then said, " the terms were *perfectly just*, and *must* be agreed to."

This answer fully exhibits that great trait in the Duke's character, that he was sincerely and faithfully attached to the interests and honours of his family; and to the lineal succession to the crown; which all must allow is best secured by the affections of the people.

His Royal Highness having heard Lord Temple's conditions, then began to state his own. The first was, that it was the King's desire that Lord Northumberland should be placed

placed at the head of the treasury. Here Lord Temple begged leave to interrupt his Royal Highness, and to say, that if this was a *positive* condition, there was no occasion to go any further. Lord Northumberland had been made Lord Lieutenant of Ireland by Lord Bute. Lord Temple answered, " That he would never go into any office under Lord Bute's Lieutenant." The determined tone in which these last words were spoken put an end to the conference.

Four days afterwards, (May 19, 1765,) his Royal Highness requested Lord Temple to meet him at Mr. Pitt's house, at Hayes in Kent. But though his Royal Highness was there first, and had had some conversation with Mr. Pitt before Lord Temple came, yet he found that Mr. Pitt and Lord Temple were one: Mr. Pitt having fully rejected the same condition, respecting Lord Northumberland.

This negotiation might have succeeded, if Lord Northumberland had not been named; but that circumstance marked the hand of

Lord Bute so strongly, it was impossible not to dread in it all the mischiefs and versatility of the continued influence of the Favourite; against which, repeated experience had shewn that the most solemn promises and protestations were no protection.

Lord Temple's firmness in these conferences with his Royal Highness did not meet with the entire approbation of some of the principal persons of the late minority: in particular the Marquis of Rockingham most ardently entreated his Lordship to accept of the Duke of Cumberland's proposals; and added, that he spoke also in the name of the Duke of Newcastle, who desired nothing for himself, but that his friends might be considered.

At this time Lord Temple and his brother, Mr. Grenville, became reconciled, through the good offices of their mutual friends; the first application was from Mr. Grenville. Neither their private honours, as gentlemen, nor their public characters, as politicians, suffered by this reconciliation. Each adhered to the opinions he had already avowed: the union

union only regarded what might occur in future. But it is very probable, that now agreeing in opinion, of the danger to every adminiſtration from the omnipotence of Lord Bute's ſecret influence, they might cordially join in any meaſure that promiſed to procure his complete overthrow.

Lord Temple's refuſal of the Duke of Cumberland's offers was aſcribed by many perſons to his reconciliation with his brother; Lord Temple would not accept, they ſaid, becauſe his brother was not included in the offers. This objection to Lord Temple's conduct, in thoſe refuſals, was repeatedly urged in various ſhapes. Sometimes in pamphlets, but oftener in letters, eſſays, and paragraphs in the public prints, until at length the opinion ſtrongly prevailed. It muſt be confeſſed, that the ſuſpicion ſeemed plauſible, and ſuch is the poſſibility of making a laſting impreſſion by reiteration, it has continued to be a ſuſpicion with ſome people even to this day. But no ſuſpicion, or opinion, could be more totally unfounded. It is only in juſtice to the memory and character of this noble Lord that the circumſtance

cumstance is mentioned, in order to undeceive those who have been misled. Lord Temple always disavowed any influence of his brother over him; and Mr. Grenville himself repeatedly desired that he might not be named to the King.

In the tract intitled " The Principles of the Changes in 1765," written under Lord Temple's own eye, and the greatest part of it dictated by him, this matter is fully explained.

" We may (says the writer) without being in Lord Temple's counsels, or pretending to unravel mysteries, safely say, he did not want inducements to accept of the great post, that presented itself as a supplicant at his gate; a post that has often been sought, but seldom, perhaps never, refused, and to him added gracious importunity to the powerful arguments of interest. One capable of such refusal cannot be supposed to be wholly destitute of that laudable ambition natural to great minds, which prompts as well as enables them to shine in elevated stations. Laying aside
the

the ties of allegiance, in a trial it is feldom put to; it were ftrange, if any fubject could be deaf to the voice, or indifferent to the wifhes of the people of England, in a diftinction fo peculiarly honourable to himfelf. Not only the noble paffions, but refentments of a lower kind, natural to humanity, if thefe were worthy of a place in fuch a confideration, might have moved him not to decline a triumph over injuries. In fhort, duty to his King, his country, as well as to himfelf, and his friends, had all their feveral claims for his acceptance. To weigh down all this, the writer (of a letter in the newfpapers) has found one motive, which he puts in the oppofite fcale; but one that, upon cool reflection, muft appear to have been the leaft capable of having any influence at all: and that is, Lord Temple's defire (as he calls it) *to save his brother, Mr. Grenville, in consequence of their reconciliation.* The chance of that was worth no price at all: and the difference of the elder brother, *without* iffue filling the office of the younger *with*, could be an object, it fhould feem, of fmall confideration between themfelves. It is not really fo hard to find

out

out the true reason of Lord Temple's refusal, as it is to assign any other that bear the test of reason. What could it be, but an apprehension of the impossibility to do his King and country that service, which an honest man would wish to do in the station he declined? His apprehensions were groundless. It is true, that Lord Bute denies that he has intermeddled since he quitted office. But why does he deny it? In defence against the charge of the late ministers, of breach of solemn engagements, he came under to them, even to remove from the King's presence, which engagements he cannot dispute. The denial has gained more credit to the assertion, than ever itself did: but it has not made the fact deemed in the least doubtful. Nobody, who knows any thing of late transactions, is ignorant that, even in public and national concerns, the late minister (Mr. Grenville) was openly thwarted by Lord Bute's friends, whenever his partial affections gave them their tone: and no influence whatever is to be seen but Lord Bute's, in the whole business of the late change. Who else could have suggested the proposition of Lord Northumberland for the head of the treasury?

treasury? and that first modest proposition is evidence cannot be required of the continued ascendant of Lord Bute, and that his aim was still to maintain an absolute dominion over this country, by being master of any ministry, to decide their fate, not according to their conduct towards the nation, but according to their submission to him. This must resolve all government into the mere arbitrary will and pleasure of the Favourite, and make the best administration that could be formed unstable as water. Who does not feel that this instability has already made us the scorn of all Europe? Nor can there be an end of it, or of its unhappy consequences, but by the annihilation of the influence of the Favourite. The title has been inauspicious in all examples; and those who now decline the service of their country, may with great propriety make their defence in the words of Charles the First's parliament, concerning the Duke of Buckingham, when they said to that unhappy King, *We protest to your Majesty, and to the whole world, that till this person be removed from intermeddling in the affairs of state, we are out of hope of any good success."*

The Duke of Cumberland's negotiation with Lord Temple having failed, his Royal Highness next applied to Lord Lyttelton. But by the advice of Lord Holland, who had many years enjoyed the confidence of his Royal Highness, the condition respecting Lord Northumberland was relinquished. His Royal Highness offered Lord Lyttelton the treasury. This change, in the complexion of the negotiation, was made too late. The original projector was discovered. Lord Lyttelton answered, that he acted in perfect coalescence with Lord Temple.

In consequence of these refusals, Lord Holland recommended to his Royal Highness, to advise his Majesty to continue his present servants. On the twenty-first of May, his Royal Highness waited on the King at the Queen's house, and having stated the answers he had received from Lord Temple, Mr. Pitt, and Lord Lyttelton, concluded with
                                                    advising

advising his Majesty to continue his present ministers.

This advice was injudicious and imprudent. Lord Holland and Lord Bute must equally suppose, that the ministers were filled with indignation and resentment, by this second attempt to dismiss them, and that one of them at least (Mr. Grenville) had adopted Lord Temple's hostility to Lord Bute.

The King followed the advice he had received from the Duke of Cumberland. He informed the subsisting ministers they were to continue in their offices. They instantly demanded the dismissions of Lord Northumberland from the lieutenancy of Ireland, of Lord Holland from the Pay-office, and of Mr. Mackenzie, Lord Bute's brother, from the Privy-seal of Scotland: and the Duke of Bedford made use of a language in the closet, that was, if possible, more provoking than these demands. There was no alternative, Lord Bute was obliged to yield. But it was only for a short time. The King himself came forward in the next negotiation. His

Majesty sent for Mr. Pitt; who waited on the King at the Queen's house, on the twentieth day of June 1765. Mr. Pitt desired to have the concurrence of Lord Temple, who was next sent for. On the twenty-fifth they waited on his Majesty together. The King proposed to put his government into their hands, upon the following conditions: The restoration of Mr. Mackenzie, the appointment of Lord Northumberland to the office of Lord Chamberlain, and all the King's friends to continue in their present places. This last condition was so undefined and unlimited, it was impossible to ascertain who it included, or who it excepted. Therefore, Lord Temple gave to the whole a decided negative; in which Mr. Pitt acquiesced.

Recourse was then had a second time to the Duke of Cumberland; who resolved to try those who had never yet been tried. These were that part of the late minority who had separated from Lord Temple.

It is not necessary in this place, to give the history of that negotiation. His Royal Highness

ness succeeded in recommending an administration, which was called the Rockingham administration, from the noble Marquis of that name being placed at the head of the treasury. But if they had not accepted of the offers of the court, the absolute and entire expulsion of Lord Bute must have been effected. The new ministers said they did not feel, nor could they discover, any symptoms of his influence. And they condemned Lord Temple's repeated refusals of the offers made to him by the Duke of Cumberland, and by the King himself, in a great number of publications, written by their friends. At length Lord Temple dictated, or nearly so, but did not write any of it himself, a pamphlet in vindication of his conduct, called "The Principles of the late Changes impartially examined;" in which a retrospect was taken from the negotiation with Mr. Pitt, in August 1763. To those who desire accurate information of this period, there are some parts of it interesting. The reader will find some extracts from it, in the Appendix, marked K.

The new ministers did not protect themselves against the manoeuvres of the court, so completely as they might have done. By an omission they committed a great fault. This omission was, not dissolving the parliament when they came in. Ample experience had shewn them the power of the court in parliament. And though, by accepting of places, they had answered the purpose of the Favourite, in the hour of his distress, yet they could not be ignorant of the want of cordiality in the court; a want, which made the necessity greater, of either diminishing the strength of the court, or increasing their own. Lord Shelburne committed the same fault in July 1782. Parliament ought to have been dissolved on both occasions.

On the great measure of the repeal of the American stamp act, which was the first parliamentary measure of the new ministers, Lord Temple adopted his brother Mr. G. Grenville's opinion. He thought that repeal was nothing short of an absolute surrender of the authority of Great Britain over the colonies.

lonies. This opinion, coinciding with that of the court, Lord Bute thought made a favourable opportunity for opening a fresh negotiation with Lord Temple, to form another administration. He first applied to Mr. W. G. Hamilton, who at that time stood so high in his Lordship's estimation, that Lord Temple had resolved to make him his Chancellor of the Exchequer, if ever he accepted of the treasury; but Mr. Hamilton gave very little encouragement to the proposition. This check did not abate Lord Bute's ardour. He next consulted Lord Eglintoun, who was one of Lord Temple's friends, and one of Mr. Grenville's also. Lord Eglintoun suggested an interview of the parties, which Lord Bute approved of. Lord Eglintoun proposed, that the parties should be Lord Bute, the Duke of Bedford, Lord Temple, and Mr. Grenville. Lord Bute objected to the Duke of Bedford. But Lord Eglintoun thought the surest way to gain Lord Temple was first to gain Mr. Grenville, which he was certain could not be accomplished, without the concurrence of the Duke of Bedford. Upon this explanation Lord Bute assented; and

Lord Eglintoun engaged to bring the parties together. Mr. Cadogan being supposed to have more influence with Mr. Grenville at this time than Lord Eglintoun, that gentleman was requested to state the matter to Mr. Grenville; which he did, and Mr. Grenville requested Lord Suffolk to acquaint the Duke of Bedford. Lord Eglintoun undertook the management of Lord Temple. But before Lord Eglintoun had an opportunity of conversing with his Lordship on the subject, Mr. Grenville had informed his brother of Lord Bute's intention, and asked him his opinion upon it. Lord Temple, in the most strong and positive terms, disclaimed for himself every possible kind of connexion with Lord Bute, immediate, remote, and eventual; but that he, his brother, might do as he pleased. This was in the month of January 1766. And when Lord Eglintoun solicited his Lordship to meet Lord Bute, at Lord Eglintoun's house, Lord Temple replied that he would not; but Lord Eglintoun pressing his request very earnestly, Lord Temple repeated his refusal in terms of warmth and indignation. Before Lord Eglintoun had opportunity to inform Lord Bute of Lord Temple's refusal, the Duke of Bedford, Lord Bute, and Mr. Grenville, came to his houfe, according to appointment. The conference was very fhort. Mr. Grenville faid afterwards in the Houfe of Commons, that their converfation was confined to one fubject, which was the repeal of the American ftamp act, and that they all agreed it was a meafure fatal to the authority of Great Britain.

Whatever was the kind of change of adminiftration which Lord Bute had in contemplation at this time, Lord Temple's refufal to fee him, or to hold any communication with him, effectually prevented the defign being attempted; for though it fhould feem that the Duke of Bedford and Mr. Grenville had no objection, yet as the party he moft wanted was not prefent, he made no propofal to them.

Lord Bute was now fully convinced, that in any future negotiation with Lord Temple or Mr. Pitt, he muft be perfectly concealed.
When

When the repeal of the American stamp act was accomplished, the miniftry made overtures to Mr. Pitt to join them, not fimply in gratitude, becaufe he had affifted them in that repeal, and without which affiftance they could not have carried it; but becaufe they were confcious of their own weaknefs, and wanted the infignia of potency, which they felt and faw he poffeffed. They offered him any fituation he would condefcend to accept. Thefe overtures alarmed Lord Bute exceedingly. He was perfectly fenfible that Mr. Pitt would not accept without Lord Temple. By the affiftance of a Great Lady at Carlton-houfe, he contrived to amufe Lord Temple, during the months of March and April 1766, with the daily expectation of a *carte blanche.* Lord Temple was for feveral weeks the dupe of this device; and notwithftanding Lord Bute's vifits at Carlton-houfe were notorious, yet this matter was fo unrefervedly declared to be totally independent of him, that had not, by accident, the " cloven foot," as Lord Temple called it, appeared unexpectedly, the deception might have been artfully continued

fome

some time longer; until perhaps some measure, or arrangement, might have been produced by it.

In the present disposition of mankind, and standing so near the time as we do, when unjust prejudices are not yet allayed, and the effects of falsehoods are not yet obliterated, a writer reluctantly offers his observation, that Lord Bute must have estimated the acquisition of Lord Temple of the utmost consequence to himself, or to the country. If he had any of that affection for the King, which the King's attachment to him had so eminently deserved, he ought, and he would, if he had been sincere, to have yielded to the happiness of his master, and the interests of the nation; and to have abandoned every thought of personal consideration. But while he remained obstinately attached to the continuation of his secret influence, Lord Temple, who was always furnished with correct information of certain secret visits and meetings, received with suspicion, and examined with jealousy every proposition that came from the court. To this sedulous attention, he owed

the

the peculiar honour of being the only English nobleman, who had not been seduced and deceived by the intrigues of Lord Bute.

During the recess of parliament, a letter written by Mr. Wilkes to Lord Temple, containing a gay account of a duel between Lord Talbot and Mr. Wilkes at Bagshot, had been published. A little time after parliament met, Lord Talbot, in a manner that was extremely abrupt, and in terms which were extremely rude, accused Lord Temple of handing this letter to the press. A duel was very near being the consequence. The seconds prevented it. Lord Talbot was mistaken in his suspicion. The letter was sent to the press by Mr. Wilkes, unknown to Lord Temple.

Notwithstanding the many disappointments Lord Bute met with in his negotiations with Lord Temple and Mr. Pitt, he was resolved to persevere, until he had gained them, or one of them at least. Accordingly, a few weeks after the close of the session of parliament, the King ordered Lord Northington, who was at that time Lord Chancellor, to send for

for Mr. Pitt. That gentleman waited upon his Majesty on the 12th day of July, at Richmond: the King told him he put himself entirely into his hands; and that he was to form such an administration as he thought proper, together with Lord Temple, who he desired might be immediately sent for.

The particulars of this negotiation having been fully and accurately stated in the "Anecdotes of the Life of Lord Chatham, Chapter xxxi." it is not necessary to repeat them here; and therefore it is only proper to observe, that after Mr. Pitt and Lord Temple had disagreed, the state of parties became exactly what Lord Bute wished.

The ministry who were dismissed to make room for the administration which had been formed by Mr. Pitt, who was now created Earl of Chatham, were attached to no set of men, they stood alone. Lord Temple, the Duke of Bedford, Mr. Grenville, and their friends, were precisely in the same situation. These

These two parties could not unite, for they held opposite opinions on the most important measures, and had so frequently and so publicly avowed those opinions they could not recede. Lord Chatham's new ministry was a motley group; it was composed of fugitives from all parties. Lord Bute's friends, or the King's friends as they were more honourably styled, continued in their several places. Thus every party was in so detached a situation, nothing formidable could be raised against him; and he could always lend his friends to the support of whatever party he chose to favour.

Lord Chatham thought, from the high authority that commenced the negotiation with him, that Lord Bute had no concern in it: but he found himself deceived. In the House of Lords on the 2d of March 1770, he publicly confessed that he had been duped, that there was something behind the throne greater than the King himself. He could not pay to Lord Temple's virtue and penetration a greater compliment.

At

At length these two great men were reconciled; but not until after Lord Chatham had quitted the court. Lord Bute enjoyed his triumph in having gained one-half of the measure he had been so long contending for. The reconciliation gave him no concern: his system at that time was too firmly established to be shaken by any party whatever.

Lord Temple continued in opposition to the measures of the court, which he considered to be those of Lord Bute, or his delegates; particularly the proceedings concerning the Middlesex election, and the war with America. His sentiments on both those subjects may be seen in the parliamentary debates. When Mr. Grenville died in the year 1770, and that gentleman's friends went over to the court, the post of Lord Privy Seal was offered to Lord Temple, which he rejected with indignation. In the year 1775 it was again signified to his Lordship that he might have it if he thought proper. But he always said, he never would wear Lord Bute's livery. His Lordship died in the year 1779.

[Some

[Some particulars in this article have so close an affinity with the anecdotes of Lord Chatham's life, that the Editor has in one or two places been under the necessity of repeating the fact in order to connect the matter.]

CHAPTER XVIII.

THE LATE RIGHT HONOURABLE GEORGE GRENVILLE.

Connection with the last Chapter. Negotiation for Peace. Sir Charles Knowles's Plan for taking the Havannah; presented to Mr. Grenville, to Lord Temple, to Mr. Pitt, to Lord Anson, to the Duke of Cumberland. Fortunate Escape of Admiral Pococke. Mr. Grenville differs with Lord Bute on demanding an Equivalent for the Havannah. Mr. Grenville removed to the Admiralty, and Lord Halifax made Secretary. Mr. Grenville complimented with a Tellership of the Exchequer for his Son. Correspondence of the Negotiation for Peace supposed to be lost. Ministers took their Papers away when removed. Mr. Grenville appointed First Lord of the Treasury. Lawyers not Politicians. Persecution of Mr. Wilkes. Lord Bute's Letter to the King. American Affairs. Project of new-modelling all the American Governments.

ments. The Outlines of the Design. True Cause of the Stamp Act. Mr. Grenville not the Author of that Act. Impolicy of it. Mr. Mauduit's Account of a Conference with Mr. Grenville. Remarks on that Paper. Governor Bernard's Letter. Trade and Connection with America explained. Mr. Gren-

pealed. The Plan of subjugating America continued. Montcalm's Letters. Mr. Grenville saves the Public Credit of all Europe. The King's Esteem for Mr. Grenville expressed upon two Occasions.

THIS Chapter follows the preceding with such particular propriety, that it may almost be called a part of it; and to be separated from it only for the sake of distinction and perspicuity. But it is not the Editor's intention to enter into the memoirs of this gentleman; but only to state some particulars of his conduct, during the present King's reign, which have either escaped the notice of other writers, or have been much misrepresented by them.

He

He was appointed Treasurer of the Navy in the late King's reign, but notwithstanding his family resigned their places in the month of October 1761, he continued in the same office until May 1762; when he was made Secretary of State in the room of the Earl of Bute, who went to the Treasury. In this situation he was necessarily a member of the cabinet, at the commencement of the negotiation for peace; which soon after followed in the same year. In the progress of this negotiation, a circumstance occurred which induced him to quit the cabinet and his office. An accommodation however was made for him with the Earl of Halifax, who was First Lord of the Admiralty, for an exchange of places: Mr. Grenville went to the Admiralty, and Lord Halifax became Secretary of State.

This circumstance was the capture of the Havannah; an acquisition that was totally unexpected. As there are some curious and interesting particulars concerning this conquest, which have not been laid before the public, it may not be improper to insert them here.

The merit of the plan of this conquest belongs to the late Admiral Sir Charles Knowles; who, in his return from Jamaica in the year 1756, prevailed on the captain of the man of war, in which he was coming home paſſenger, to put in at the Havannah. Admiral Knowles's ſtimulation at that moment was no more than curioſity, to obtain a view of this celebrated place. Being a time of peace with Spain, he was permitted to go through all the fortifications, and through all parts of the town and environs.——A few weeks previous to Mr. Pitt's reſignation, which was in the early part of the month of October 1761, when a war with Spain was ſuppoſed to be more than probable, Sir Charles made a correct copy of all his plans and papers, taken and written upon the ſpot, relative to the Havannah, and recommended in a very ſtrong memorial an immediate attack upon that place, in caſe of a war. Theſe plans and papers he put into the hands of Mr. Grenville, accompanied with a requeſt to recommend them to Mr. Pitt. But Mr. Grenville, in order to give the project the beſt ſupport he could, begged leave to refer it to Lord Temple, his Lordſhip being more in the confidence

fidence of Mr. Pitt than any other person. Lord Temple highly approved of the proposal, and gave to it his warmest recommendation to Mr. Pitt. A war with Spain was not at this moment quite certain; yet very nearly so: but Mr. Pitt so eagerly embraced the whole plan, that in case the war with Spain had commenced during his continuance in power, his fixed determination was, to have ordered the fleet and army he had sent against Martinico, as soon as they had reduced that island, to go immediately against the Havannah; and to have sent to them timely reinforcements sufficient to ensure the success. And in order to have every necessary preparation ready for the undertaking, he sent the papers to Lord Anson, at that time First Lord of the Admiralty. But the expulsion of Lord Temple and Mr. Pitt from the State following almost immediately after these consultations, the plan and the design lay dormant; until Sir Charles Knowles some time after the war against Spain had been declared, sent another copy of the whole of his papers to the Duke of Cumberland: thus the matter revived. Notwithstanding the entire approbation, and the

the respectability of those great persons who had recommended this plan yet Lord Anson declared it to be in many parts injudicious and improper: he therefore framed another; or at least new-modelled the first. But the delay and unwillingness manifest in executing every part of the plan, were very nearly proving fatal to the expedition. Mr. Pitt's idea of sending the force from Martinico was adopted; but with a most malicious view. The reinforcements sent from England, consisting of only four ships of the line and four regiments, did not sail from Portsmouth until the month of March 1762; though they might and ought to have sailed six weeks sooner; and consequently would have arrived before the sickly season, by which they suffered dreadfully, and would have found the Spaniards almost unprepared. But what is most extraordinary, and wholly inexplicable, is, that when they arrived at Martinico, they were ordered, in case that island was not subdued, to abandon the attempt, and to take away the whole of the British force there, and proceed to the Havannah. But it fortunately happened, that General Monckton had completed

the

the conqueſt of Martinico before Lord Albemarle arrived; and thereby the hopes of riage at Martinico were diſappointed. There was another circumſtance not leſs fortunate: when Admiral Pococke ſailed from England with the four ſhips and the four regiments, the French had a fleet of twelve ſail of the line lying at Cape François, under the command of M. Blenac. If the French officer had been vigilant, he might have intercepted Admiral Pococke and captured him; and why he did not, was the ſurpriſe of every body in France and England at that time.

When the intelligence of the conqueſt of the Havannah arrived in London, which was in the month of October 1762, the negotiations for peace between France, Spain, and England were far advanced; and many, if not all the principal conditions were agreed upon: but a very extraordinary negligence, or ſomething worſe, appeared in theſe negotiations; for though all the powers knew of the expedition gone againſt the Havannah, yet no mention was made of it in the negotiation.

tiation. It seems to have been understood, confidentially no doubt, that whatever might be the event of the expedition, it should make no change in the conditions of peace; it was to be restored, if taken. It is only in this manner that the conduct of Lord Bute on this point can be explained. Fortunately the preliminaries were not signed when the news came. In the first council after the receipt of the intelligence, Mr. Grenville immediately proposed that the Havannah should be included in the *uti possidetis*. Lord Bute insisted that the negotiation was too far advanced to admit of any alteration; that though the event was in our favour, yet he very much dreaded that our making any fresh demand on this account would prevent the peace taking place for some time. Mr. Grenville said he did not object to restoring the Havannah to Spain; all he contended was, that Spain or France, or both, should make a compensation for it: either Porto Rico and St. Lucie, or Florida and the entire property of Jucatan, should be demanded for it. Lord Bute refused to consent to either of these propositions being made: upon which

Mr.

Mr. Grenville declared his resolution of quitting the cabinet; and, upon an accommodation being made with Lord Halifax, he went to the Admiralty; which removed him from all farther concern with the negotiation. However, Lord Bute, in a very little time, either changed his sentiments, or began to be afraid of the consequences, as he thought proper to make the demand of Florida only; which was readily granted. But if the interests of Great Britain had been considered, Porto Rico and Jucatan were infinitely preferable; and if any estimation is to be put on the facility of gaining Florida, it will not be doubted that Porto Rico, Jucatan, and St. Lucie might also have been obtained if they had been firmly insisted upon. Spain would have bought the Havannah at any price; and perhaps she gave more for it than the world is yet acquainted with.

Mr. Grenville's accommodation on this point did not pass without its reward. He was complimented with the reversion of the first vacant tellership of the Exchequer, for his eldest son; who succeeded to it in the month of April 1763, upon the death of Lord Waldegrave.

There

There were several other parts of the treaty of peace with France and Spain not less interesting to the public; and had the correspondence relative to the negotiation been laid before parliament, which it ought to have been, a clue to certain transactions might have been found, that would have led to some discoveries which might have astonished the British nation, and perhaps all Europe. But probably this correspondence is not now in existence; or if it should be found, it is probable that it will be in some private scrutoire; for at this time the cabinet ministers considered all their official correspondence as their private papers, and their own property; and when they or any of them quitted their situations, they took from the offices all such original papers and letters as had come there during their administration. This practice might be prudent, in the apprehension of consequences, but it was unjust to the government, and to the country.

When Lord Bute resigned the place of First Lord of the Treasury, which has been explained in the preceding Chapter, Mr. Grenville

ville was appointed his fucceffor on the 16th of April 1763: the fortuitous circumftances of the times placed him in this fituation; which, though he filled with integrity and unblemifhed honour, as a gentleman, he wanted that fpecies of genius which is moft ufeful to a minifter—a comprehenfive mind. He had been bred to the law; and had he been permitted to continue in that line, there is no vain opinion hazarded in offering a probable conjecture, that he would have committed to pofterity a more honourable character than either Lord Hardwicke or Lord Mansfield. But Lord Cobham thought otherwife, and made him a ftatefman: when his Lordfhip joined the Pelhams in the year 1744, Mr. Grenville was made a Lord of the Admiralty; therefore he could no longer appear at the bar. But there is fomething in the habit or practice of the gentlemen of the law, which feems to confine the mind to diftinct points; whether it is from the cafes of individuals claiming their daily attention, or the peculiar contraction of their ftudies, certain it is, that fcarcely one lawyer in an age can be called a politician, though fo many affume

the

the name. They are too apt to limit their principles and ideas to the focus of an act of parliament. In the great debate on the repeal of the American stamp act, Mr. Grenville maintained the narrow ground of a legislative authority: Lord Chatham took the broad ground of constitutional right.

Even Mr. Knox, who had obligations to Mr. Grenville, and was consequently partial to him, speaks very coldly of his general knowledge. His words are these:—" He (Mr. Grenville) was not well acquainted with the internal state of Ireland; and he knew still less of the circumstances of the American colonies." This is not very like the language of a friend, whatever it may be of candour.

The principal features of Mr. Grenville's administration are the persecution of Mr. Wilkes, and the oppression of North America: neither of which can, perhaps, be strictly called his own. But it was not until after his death that it was authentically known these measures had not originated with himself; that they had been suggested to him by others
—by

—by the confidents of Carlton-houfe, and the confidents of Lord Bute. So true it is, that minifters have often been feduced into paths, without feeing the hand that led them. He had too much of referve in his temper, and of what the French call *hauteur* in his manner, to open himfelf freely, even to his friends; fo that he became his own enemy as to his real difpofition, and wholly fo in bearing the odium of thefe meafures.

In the perfecution of Mr. Wilkes he was probably fincere. That gentleman had treated him with fome feverity, on account of his having attached himfelf firft to Lord Bute, and afterwards to the Duke of Bedford; and thereby having totally feparated himfelf from his family. They felt the lofs of him; and therefore could not ftomach what they naturally called a defertion of them. In families, thefe divifions, though not of a private nature, are too frequently fpoken of in terms of acrimony. The friends of the parties are too prone to adopt the language of the principals; which, in the courfe of circulation, foon reaches the ears of minifters, who never

forget

forget, the *divide et impera*, nor to practife, improve, and apply the cafe of the moment to the exifting circumftances of the period. It is a matter extremely to be regretted, that political perfecutions in England have feldom had their true foundation in the pretended crime affigned. They have originated in fome perfonality, or oppofition to fome line of politics purfued by the Minifter. The perfecution of the North Briton was generally fuppofed to have been occafioned by the *fifth* number of that paper, which was publifhed many months before Mr. Grenville became Minifter.

In the firft overtures of the negotiation, which Lord Bute opened with Mr. Pitt, in the month of Auguft 1763, he fhewed a partiality for Mr. Grenville. His firft propofition was to continue him at the head of the treafury: but Mr. Pitt would not confent to it. Lord Bute finding that his plan of a coalition was impracticable, had recourfe to the expedient of introducing Mr. Pitt to the King, who propofed Lord Northumberland for the treafury; to which Mr. Pitt alfo refufed

fufed his affent. The negotiation broke off, and Mr. Grenville was entreated by the King to continue in his fituation. The minifters were exceedingly offended with Lord Bute for his attempt to difplace them. The notoriety of the fact revived and confirmed the general fufpicion of Lord Bute's fecret influence. Upon this occafion it was that Lord Bute wrote a letter to the King, foliciting his Majefty's permiffion to withdraw himfelf from all public and private counfels. One of Lord Bute's friends, who feems to have been well-informed, has given the following account of this letter :

He wrote a letter to his gracious Sovereign, " humbly ftating the refolution which, for the King's fervice as well as for his own eafe, he had thought himfelf obliged to take: and then to remove all occafions of jealoufy, he retired to his houfe in Bedfordfhire for the whole enfuing winter 1763-4. The letter gave Mr. Grenville no claim to expect of the Earl of Bute his retirement from the concerns of ftate; no right to complain of breach of faith, if he fhould afterwards have ftepped stepped forwards, and been received by the crown into the management of affairs, either open and avowed, or secret and confidential; because that letter had nothing in it of the nature of a compact with Mr. Grenville or any other person. The letter was not written until after Mr. Grenville had agreed to stay in the King's service. There was a passage in the letter which expresly mentioned Mr. Grenville's determination to keep his employment, as an event that had actually taken place. The letter, as I have said, was declaratory of the Earl of Bute's wish and intention to withdraw from the King's business, for reasons which concerned the quiet of his Majesty's government, as well as the repose of the Earl of Bute himself." *Interesting Letters, vol.* ii. *page* 69. *edit.* 1767.

There needs no stronger proof of Lord Bute's secret influence than this letter. He resolves upon a temporary absence from the capital, to his own house, very little more than thirty miles distant, with the silly hope of changing appearances. He renounces nothing: on the contrary, his advocate says, that

that it is no breach of faith, if he fhould ftep forward again in the management of affairs, either open and avowed, or fecret and confidential. The laft Chapter is the fulleft commentary on the text.

With regard to the affairs of America, Mr. Grenville had no concern whatever in the firft caufes of the difquietudes there. They originated in the projects which were formed while Lord Bute was in office. It was obvious, from the fucceffes of the war, that the continent of North America muft belong to Great Britain. A plan was recommended by a naval officer from Bofton, of new-modelling the governments of that country. This fcheme commenced, in idea, before the conclufion of the peace in 1763. The project was flattering to the Minifter, becaufe it gave him an immenfe increafe of patronage, and if any caufe can be affigned for his preferring Florida to Porto Rico, it muft be the further increafe of patronage, and making Florida into two governments. A junto of fycophants and confidents, whom Lord Bute encouraged, and with whom he principally advifed, vised, eagerly embraced this project of distributing the American revenues amongst their relations and dependents.

When the peace was concluded, the British army was not withdrawn. Several pretences were made for keeping it in America; such as an Indian war, and the necessity of having garrisons in the back settlements. The first measure was a division of the country into military districts, with a brigadier-general in each, all of them depending upon the commander in chief, who was totally independent of the civil power.

This scheme of new-modelling the governments in America, in order to increase the power and patronage of the crown, was the sole cause of the war, and the loss of America. It is true, that occasional circumstances were the immediate causes of particular events; but it is always to be remembered, that those circumstances, and every instruction sent to America, from the resignation of Mr. Pitt in the month of October 1761, to the defeat of General Burgoyne in the month of October 1777,

1777, originated in the great defign of rendering America fubfervient to the purpofes of the Minifter.

The prominent features of the grand plan were thefe: Firft, to raife a revenue in America by act of parliament, to be applied to fupport an army, to pay a large falary to the governor, another to the lieutenant-governor, falaries to the judges of the law and admiralty: thus, the whole government, executive and judicial, was to be rendered entirely independent of the people, and wholly dependent on the Minifter. Second, to make a new divifion of the colonies, to reduce the number of them by making the fmall ones more extenfive, to make them all royal governments, with an ariftocracy in each. This order of ariftocrats was not intended to be hereditary, but fomething like the Lords of Seffion in Scotland, for life only. But in a little time they would doubtlefs have become hereditary, like the nobility of France, whofe origin is fimilar. See the article in the Appendix marked L. Amherft was the firft perfon who fuggefted the idea of an American peerage;

peerage; at one time he had thoughts of being created an American peer, with precedency of all others.

In order to support this military system, which was only the basis of the plan, it was necessary to create a fund to establish a revenue, which would soon have been followed by a system of corruption. This gave rise to the American stamp act.

The American stamp act forms the other principal feature of Mr. Grenville's administration. The great zeal with which he defended this act, gave rise to a general opinion that the act was his own measure; and it was not until near seven years after his death that the public were undeceived in this matter. On the fifteenth day of May in the year 1777, Mr. Charles Jenkinson, who had been private secretary to Lord Bute, and is now Earl of Liverpool, said in the House of Commons, " That the measure of the stamp act was not Mr. Grenville's; if the act was a good one, the merit of it was not due to Mr. Grenville; if it was a bad one, the

errors

errors or the ill policy of it did not belong to him."

Whether the account of the speech is perfectly correct, as to the exact words of it, may be uncertain: but it is unquestionably true, that the speech assured the House, that Mr. Grenville was not the author of the stamp act. He adopted it, because it was agreeable to his ideas of raising a revenue in America. Those who flattered him with this unhappy notion, were refugees from America, who were driven from thence for misconduct, and who, in motives of resentment, offered their several plans for distressing America. Unfortunately this project of a stamp act was adopted, without reflecting that a greater revenue was obtaining from America by an increasing trade, and an increasing population, than was practicable by any direct mode of receiving it. Commerce gave it copiously, but circuitously; and though this abundantly increased the wealth of both countries, and, as Lord Chatham said, carried us triumphantly through the great seven years war, yet it was not intelligible to the country gentlemen, nor so flattering to the friends of prerogative, as the patronage of an army of revenue officers.

Although Mr. Grenville fell into this fatal system, yet he was not at first particularly attached to the measure of the stamp act. His ardent desire was to gain a revenue from America. His wishes went no further; and as to the mode, he was then indifferent to it, whether it was by stamps or any thing else. In the month of March 1764, he proposed in the Committee of Supply a number of resolutions concerning America; one of which was this stamp act; the other resolutions all passed, but this was put off till next year. At the end of the session, the American agents went to him in a body. Of the conference which took place between the Minister and the agents, Mr. Israel Mauduit has given an account; but as the paper is in few hands, it will not be improper to print it here.

" I shall give a plain narration of facts, which fell within my own knowledge, and which I think it a debt due from me to Mr. Grenville's memory to relate.

" In

" In the beginning of March 1764, a number of resolutions, relative to the plantation trade, were proposed by Mr. Grenville, and passed in the House of Commons.

" The fifteenth of these was: '.That, to-
' wards the further defraying the said ex-
' pences, it may be proper to charge certain
' stamp duties in the said colonies and plant-
' ations.'

[The agent for Georgia, in his account of this conference with Mr. Grenville, explains this resolution in these words: " In the year 1764, the colonies were made acquainted through their agents, that a revenue would be required from them, *towards defraying the charge of the troops kept up among them.*"]

" The other resolutions were formed into the plantation act: but the fifteenth was put off till the next session: Mr. Grenville declaring, that he was willing to give time to the colonies to consider of it, and to make their option of raising that, or some other tax. The agents waited separately on Mr. Grenville upon this matter, and wrote to their several colonies. At the end of the sessions we went to him, all of us together, to know if he still intended to bring in such a bill. He answered, he did; and then repeated to us in form, what I had before heard him say in private, and in the House of Commons: 'That the 'late war had found us seventy millions, and 'left us more than one hundred and forty 'millions in debt. He knew that all men 'wished not to be taxed; but that in these un- 'happy circumstances, it was his duty, as a 'steward for the public, to make use of every 'just means of improving the public revenue: 'that he never meant, however, to charge 'the colonies with any part of the interest of 'the national debt. But, besides that public 'debt, the nation had incurred a great annual 'expence in the maintaining of the several 'new conquests, which we had made during 'the war, and by which the colonies were so 'much benefited. That the American civil 'and military establishment, after the peace 'of Aix-la-Chapelle, was only 70,000*l.* per 'ann. It was now increased to 350,000*l.* 'This was a great additional expence incurred

'upon

' upon an American account: and he thought,
' therefore, that America ought to contribute
' towards it. He did not expect that the
' colonies should raise the whole; but some
' part of it he thought they ought to raise.
' And this stamp duty was intended for that
' purpose.

' That he judged this method of raising
' the money the easiest and most equitable;
' that it was a tax which would fall only
' upon property; would be collected by the
' fewest officers; and would be equally spread
' over America and the West Indies; so that
' all would bear their share of the public
' burden.'

" He then went on: ' I am not, however,
' set upon this tax: if the Americans dislike
'
' the money themselves, I shall be content.
' Write therefore to your several colonies;
' and if they choose any other mode, I shall
' be satisfied, provided the money be but
' raised.'

" Upon

"Upon reading over this narration with Mr. Montagu, who was then agent for Virginia, and present at this conference with Mr. Grenville, I have his authority to say, that he entirely assents to every particular.

"All these particulars I had before heard from Mr. Grenville, in the House of Commons, and at his own house; and had wrote to the Massachuset's assembly accordingly,

"The following extracts contain their answer on this head:

'SIR, Boston, June 14, 1764.
'The House of Representatives have re-
'ceived your several letters, &c. * * *
* * * * * * * *
* * * *

'The actual laying the stamp duty, you
'say, is deferred till next year, Mr. Grenville
'being willing to give the provinces their
'option to raise that, or some equiva-
'lent tax; desirous, as he was pleased
'to express himself, "to consult the case
'and

' and quiet, and the good-will of the
' colonies."

" 'If the ease, the quiet, and the good-will
' of the colonies are of any importance to
' Great Britain, no measures could be hit
' upon, that have a more natural and direct
' tendency to enervate those principles, than
' the resolutions you inclosed.

' The kind offer of suspending this stamp
' duty in the manner, and upon the condi-
' tion you mention, amounts to no more than
' this, that if the colonies will not tax them-
' selves, as they may be directed, the parlia-
' ment will tax them.

' You are to remonstrate against these mea-
' sures, and, if possible, to obtain a repeal of
' the sugar act, and prevent the imposition of
' any further duties or taxes on the colonies.
' Measures will be taken that you may be
' joined by all the other agents.'

" One of these measures was the printing
this letter, and sending it the other colony
assemblies.

" After

" After their own exprefs acknowledgment therefore, no one, I fuppofe, will doubt, but that they had the offer of raifing the money themfelves; and that they refufed it. Which is all that I am concerned to prove.

ISRAEL MAUDUIT."

This paper is infidious. The infinuation is obvious; it is this, that America refufed to give any aid or affiftance to Great Britain: no infinuation could be more unjuft than it was. Becaufe the Americans refufed to tax themfelves in the year 1764, when they were deeply in debt, does it follow that they never would comply with *any requifition* from the mother country? They often had done it. The point in difpute was, *not* whether the Americans would be taxed, but whether they fhould be taxed as the Britifh and Irifh are, by an affembly chofen by themfelves; or by an affembly in which they never had a fingle reprefentative. At the time the ftamp act was paffed, America was in fuch a fituation as made the attempt to tax her, not lefs *unjuft* than impolitic: the teftimony of Governor Bernard upon this fubject is decifive. The following extracts are made from his ninth letter:

" Bofton,

"Boston, Nov. 23, 1765.

".......... "A little consideration would have made it *at least doubtful*, whether an inland taxation of the Americans was practicable or *equitable* at this time. If I had had the question put to me, I think I should have proved the negative in both particulars. It must have been supposed, that such an *innovation* as a parliamentary taxation would cause a great alarm, and meet with much opposition in most parts of America. *It was quite new to the people, and had no visible bounds set to it.* The Americans declared they would not submit to it before the act passed; and there was the greatest probability that it would require the utmost power of government to carry it into execution......... Was this a time to introduce so great a novelty as a parliamentary inland taxation into America? Nor was the time less favourable to the *equity* of such a taxation. I don't mean to dispute the reasonableness of America contributing to the charges of Great Britain, when she is *able*; nor, *I believe, would the Americans themselves have disputed it at a proper time and season.*

But

But it should be considered that the American governments themselves have, in the prosecution of the late war, *contracted very large debts*, which it will take some years to pay off, and in the mean time occasion *very burdensome taxes* for that purpose only. For instance, this government, which is as much beforehand as any, raises every year thirty-seven thousand five hundred pounds sterling, for sinking their debt, and must continue it for four years longer, at least, before it will be clear. .... It were much to be wished that America could be brought to the state it was in two years ago, when there was a general disposition to submit to regulations and *requisitions,* necessary to the reformation of the governments, and ascertaining their relation to Great Britain. But that time is *past*, and *not to be retrieved.*"

Without entering into the wisdom, the policy, or the interest of the American stamp act, which would now be nugatory, and labour lost; it may not be unuseful, as history, to add, that Great Britain had confined all the American trade to herself; that the Americans had

had submitted to this limitation, because it was for the general good of the empire. And here it would be uncandid not to admit their argument, in the way of balance, to the charge made against them of refusing to be taxed. They said that they ought to be allowed as credit, in the account of the national income and expences, the sum of money which they lost by being obliged to sell their commodities *cheaper* to Great Britain, than they could get for them at foreign markets: this difference they averred was a tax upon America, for the good of the empire. They were obliged likewise to take commodities from Great Britain, which they could purchase *cheaper* elsewhere. This difference they insisted was also a tax upon America for the good of the empire. And they further asserted, that three millions of Americans, (which at that time was the supposed number of them advanced to the state of maturity,) by being obliged to export to Great Britain only, and to import from Great Britain only; and the quantities of British manufactures which they consumed, ultimately paid more taxes and duties than any three millions of persons in Great Britain or Ireland; and they appealed to the public accounts for the truth of this assertion.

If the features of this very short statement are acknowledged to be those of justice and truth, it must follow, that the impolicy of attempting to tax America, at this time, is established: but here it is to be remembered that policy made no part of the consideration. A great design had been formed of altering the government of America, and this distinct measure was only a *gradus* in the elevation. Mr. Grenville was the dupe of the designers, without perceiving it. His idea was to gain a *revenue* from America, it went no further: but their idea was to make a *new conquest* of America, which extended to every thing, and did not leave to the inhabitants any thing which they could call their own. If this plan had succeeded, the Americans would have been as absolute slaves to the minions of Lord Bute, as the English were to the soldiers of William the Conqueror.

In the year 1765 Mr. Grenville was removed from the administration, in the manner that

that has been related in the preceding Chapter; and many of the subsequent events having also been related in the preceding Chapter, it is not necessary to repeat them here. In the year 1766, during the administration of the Marquis of Rockingham, the stamp act was repealed, not with a view of crushing the intended colonial system, but as a measure of expediency to restore tranquillity. The ministry do not seem to have viewed the stamp act as a part of a plan of subjugation; but Lord Chatham seems to have viewed it in that light, when he said, (in the debate upon the repeal,) " I rejoice that America has resisted. Three millions of people so dead to all the feelings of liberty as to submit to be slaves, would have been fit instruments to make slaves of the rest."

In the same session that the stamp act was passed, another bill was introduced, making it lawful for military officers in the colonies to quarter their soldiers in *private* houses. This was indisputably with a view of enforcing the grand design of entire subjugation. The colonists were all alarmed: the agents and

American merchants all opposed it, declaring, that under such a military power no one could look upon his house as his own, or think he had a home, when soldiers might be thrust into it, and mix with his family, at the pleasure of an officer: upon which this part of the bill was dropt. But there was another clause in it which obliged the assemblies to find quarters for the soldiers, and to furnish them with firing, bedding, candles, beer, rum, and other articles, at the expence of the colony, which passed into a law; and was not repealed with the stamp act.

Notwithstanding there were frequent changes of ministers in the subsequent years, yet the junto of confidants, who had been originally entrusted with a plan against America, persevered throughout every administration, (except Lord Chatham's,) in making advances towards the attainment of the grand object; until at length the colonies were driven into rebellion, independence, and separation. Philip the Second lost the Netherlands in the same manner.

Assurances

Assurances were made to Mr. Grenville, that America had entertained thoughts of independency so early as the year 1757; and to confirm these assurances, some letters, written, it was asserted, by the Marquis de Montcalm, Governor of Canada, in the years 1757, 1758, and 1759, stating these opinions, were put into his hands. Mr. Grenville gave full credit to these papers: after his death they were published. All the Americans reprobated them as forgeries, they insisted that Montcalm never wrote them, that they were fabricated to deceive and provoke the English government against America. This opinion prevailed with the public, and the letters were in general discredited.

There is another circumstance of Mr. Grenville's administration which it may not be improper to take notice of.

A little time after the conclusion of the war, the base money which had been coined, and forced into circulation during the war, by the King of Prussia, and some other powers, having come into the hands of merchants, bankers, and traders, who had been obliged to receive it, the depreciation of it, on the return of peace, fell upon, and ruined many of them; and would have extended the same fate to many more; and to several in England, who were connected with the houses in Amsterdam, Hamburgh, and Berlin, which were the greatest sufferers, had not Mr. Grenville zealously interposed with his whole weight and authority, as minister, in their favour. He requested the British merchants to give a liberal credit to the houses abroad, which were injured by this depression, and instead of limiting, to increase their exports to them; and he requested of the Governors and Directors of the Bank of England, to give their full countenance to the English houses by an ample discount of bills. By thus lending the assistance of the British government in a critical hour, he stopped the alarm of a general failure, which might spread throughout Europe in a very little time. Mr. Grenville was entitled to great praise for the personal exertions he made in this important business. It may be truly said of him, that he saved the credit of almost every bank in Europe.

Mr.

Mr. Grenville's spirited behaviour on the French seizing Turk's Island in the year 1764, his Navy bill, his bill for trying controverted elections, together with several other circumstances of his conduct, are traits of his character, which reflect great honour on his memory as a minister, and particularly as a legislator. But these matters have been all stated in other books, and it is not the design of this work to repeat what has been already printed; except the extracts and papers in the Appendix, which are explanatory and scarce.

Two months after his decease, which happened in the month of November 1770, several of his friends, who had been attached to him in the hopes of his return to power, offered themselves to Lord North, and were accepted. When the Earl of Suffolk came to kiss hands on being appointed Lord Privy Seal, the King soothed him, with saying, " That he lamented very much the loss of his Lordship's friend, that great and good man Mr. Grenville, who was an honour to human nature." And upon another occasion, the

King expressed the same sentiments of Mr. Grenville: this was on the delivery of the Spanish rescript in the month of June 1779; when his Majesty ordered all his cabinet ministers to attend him at the Queen's House in St. James's Park. They were shewn into the library, where there was a long table, and chairs for every one of them, and an armed chair at the top for himself. They were desired to be seated, which being done, his Majesty made a long speech to them. He began with expressing his regard for Mr. Grenville, and his concern for the loss of him; and afterwards declared his resolution to carry on the war against America, France, and Spain; and if they approved of it, he gave them an assurance of his firmest support. They all acknowledged their perfect devotion to his Majesty's commands.

CHAPTER XIX.

THOMAS WHATELY, Esq.

His Tracts. Letters to him from Governor Hutchinson and Lieutenant Governor Oliver, shewn to different Persons; sent to America by Dr. Franklin. Resolutions in America upon them. Petition to remove the Governor and Lieutenant Governor. Duel between Mr. Temple and Mr. William Whately.

THIS gentleman was Secretary to the Treasury during Mr. Grenville's administration. He was the author of two tracts written in defence of Mr. Grenville.

The first was called " Remarks on the Budget." A pamphlet had been published, called " The Budget," which contained a severe attack on Mr. Grenville's measures of finance, and the Remarks were a defence of those measures in answer to it.

The other tract was called " Confiderations on the Trade and Finances of this Kingdom, and on the Meafures of Adminiftration, with refpect to thofe great National Objects fince the Conclufion of the Peace." This is another defence of Mr. Grenville's fyftem of finance, and of the principal meafures of his adminiftration, in which there is a good deal of ufeful information.

The moft remarkable circumftance concerning this gentleman is relative to his American correfpondence, on account of the confequences which attended it. In the years 1767, 1768, and 1769, Thomas Hutchinfon, Efq. Governor of Maffachufetts Bay, and Andrew Oliver, Efq. Lieutenant Governor, wrote feveral letters to Mr. Whately, giving very full accounts of the ftate of the province, the difpofitions of the principal inhabitants, the meafures which they conceived moft proper to be taken, and their own opinions and fentiments upon all thefe at confiderable length. The fubjects of all thefe letters being the public affairs of America, which at that time engaged the public attention in England,

and

and being written by perſons in high authority, Mr. Whately ſhewed them to Mr. Grenville, who ſhewed them to Lord Temple, and they were ſeen by other gentlemen. When Mr. Whately died, which was in the month of June 1772, theſe letters came into the poſſeſſion of a gentleman, who put them into the hands of Dr. Franklin, at that time agent for the province of which they gave ſo full an account: Dr. Franklin ſent them to the Speaker of the Houſe of Repreſentatives of Maſſachuſetts Bay. In the month of June 1773, the Speaker laid them before the Houſe. On reading them, the Houſe was highly offended with the Governor and Lieutenant Governor; ſeveral ſtrong reſolutions againſt them were agreed to; two or three of which will be ſufficient to quote, to ſhew the ſenſe of the Houſe.

" Reſolved, That it clearly appears from the letters ſigned Tho. Hutchinſon and Andrew Oliver, that it was the deſire and endeavour of the writers of them, that certain acts of the Britiſh Parliament for raiſing a revenue in America might be carried into effect by military

military force. That there have been for many years past measures contemplated, and a plan formed by a set of men, born and educated among us, to raise their own fortunes, and advance themselves to posts of honour and profit, not only to the destruction of the constitution of this province, but at the expence of the rights and liberties of the American colonies. That the said persons have been some of the chief instruments in the introduction of a military force into the province to carry their plans into execution. That this House is bound in duty to the King and their constituents, humbly to remonstrate to his Majesty the conduct of his Excellency Thomas Hutchinson, Esq. Governor, and the Honourable Andrew Oliver, Esq. Lieutenant Governor of this province, and to pray that his Majesty would be pleased to remove them for ever from the government thereof."

Conformable to the last resolution, the House agreed to a petition to the King to remove the Governor and Lieutenant Governor for writing the letters to Mr. Whately. This petition was heard before the Privy Council

Council at Whitehall, on the 29th day of January 1774; when it was difmiffed after a long fpeech made by Mr. Wedderburne, now Lord Loughborough, in defence of the Governor and Lieutenant Governor, in which he reproached Dr. Franklin with great feverity and bitternefs for fending the letters to America.

When it was known in England that the letters to Mr. Whately had been laid before the Houfe of Reprefentatives of Maffachufetts Bay, the fufpicion of fending them to America fell upon Mr. John Temple, an American gentleman at that time in England; and there were fome circumftances, which, before they were explained, feemed to give foundation to the fufpicion. This matter brought on a duel between Mr. Temple and Mr. William Whately brother of Mr. Thomas Whately. As the circumftances were fingular, the reader will find an account of them in the Appendix, marked M.

Mr. Whately alfo wrote a tract on laying out pleafure grounds and gardens.

CHAPTER XX.

CHARLES LLOYD, Esq.

Names of the Tracts written by him.

THIS gentleman was private secretary to Mr. Grenville, during the time that gentleman was First Lord of the Treasury, and author of many political tracts, chiefly written in vindication of that minister's conduct. They were principally the following:

" The Anatomy of a late Negotiation." The negotiation here spoken of, is that which Lord Bute brought on between the King and Mr. Pitt, in the autumn of the year 1763. The facts are purposely misrepresented, to make Mr. Pitt appear haughty and Lord Bute versatile.

" A Vindication of the Conduct of the Ministry in the case of Mr. Wilkes." This
relates

relates to the apprehension of Mr. Wilkes by the general warrant, his commitment to the Tower, and his discharge by the Court of Common Pleas; highly commending the ministry for their zeal in defending the honour of the King.

" A Defence of the Majority in the House of Commons, on the Question relating to General Warrants." This was an answer to Mr. Townshend's Defence of the Minority on the same question. It was in reply to this Defence of the Majority that the celebrated " Letter on Libels and Warrants" was writtten.

" An Honest Man's Reasons for declining to take a Part in the New Administration." This was the administration of 1765, commonly called the Rockingham Administration. The reasons assigned are, that Lord Bute removed the late ministry, and in a little time would remove the present. It was ascribed very generally to Lord Lyttelton, because his Lordship had refused the offers which were made to him.

" A Cri-

"A Critical Review of the New Administration." This is an answer to two pamphlets written by Sir Grey Cooper; one was called "A Pair of Spectacles for short-sighted Politicians;" the other, "The Merits of the New Administration truly stated." See the article of Sir Grey Cooper.

"The Conduct of the late Administration examined, relative to the Repeal of the American Stamp Act." This tract (which is upwards of two hundred pages) is an able composition, and the greatest part of it, if not all of it, was dictated by Mr. Grenville himself. Those persons who wish to see a defence of the stamp act, and a display of what the writer considers the impolicy of repealing it, will read this work with pleasure.

Mr. Burke having written a little tract called "A short Account of a late short Administration," Mr. Lloyd wrote an answer to it, which was called "A true History of a late short Administration." These small tracts contain all the features of the Rockingham administration in miniature.

"An

" An Examination of the Principles and boasted Disinterestedness of a late Right Hon. Gentleman; in a Letter from an old Man of Business to a Noble Lord." This tract was written upon the change of the ministry in the year 1766, when Mr. Pitt, who is the right honourable gentleman alluded to, was created Earl of Chatham. The noble Lord to whom it is pretended to be a letter was Lord North. It is a vindication of Lord Temple's conduct in rejecting the offers of the court, and blames Lord Chatham for accepting them.

" A Word at Parting, to his Grace the Duke of Bedford." This small tract was occasioned by the Duke of Bedford's friends joining the ministry at the end of the year 1767, and abandoning Mr. Grenville.

Besides these, he wrote many Essays and Letters in the public papers, on political temporary subjects, which are now lost. He was brother to the Dean of Norwich.

CHAPTER XXI.

WILLIAM KNOX, Esq.

Advocate for the American War. Secretary to Lord George Germaine. His State of the Nation; assisted by Mr. Grenville. Other Publications.

THIS gentleman was another of Mr. Grenville's friends; and was a very strenuous and persevering advocate of the British measures against America. He was agent for Georgia; and Under Secretary of State to Lord Hillsborough, and to Lord George Germaine, during the American war. To his zeal and suggestions, many of the unfortunate measures against America were ascribed, and he sustained much hatred from the Americans on that account. He was the author of several tracts on American subjects, the principal of which was,

" The

"The Controverſy between Great Britain and her Colonies reviewed." It is obviouſly a work of much labour, and contains extracts from many papers. The writer's view is to ſupport the right of Great Britain to tax America.

He was alſo the writer of a tract intitled "The Preſent State of the Nation; particularly with reſpect to its Trade, Finances, &c." This pamphlet was, at firſt, aſcribed to Mr. Grenville; and Mr. Burke, by his pamphlet intitled "Obſervations upon it," gave a temporary currency to that opinion. Mr. Grenville undoubtedly aſſiſted the writer with materials and arguments, but the compoſition belongs entirely to Mr. Knox. It conſiſts principally of a defence of Mr. Grenville's miniſtry and meaſures, and a condemnation of the Rockingham' miniſtry, and their meaſures.

Mr. Knox has alſo publiſhed two ſmall volumes, called "Extra-official State Papers;" which contain many uſeful hints.

The two following Letters are not unworthy of the reader's notice:

"Sir,   5th March 1783.

"Letters having been written to the Secretary of the late Board of Trade, and to my colleague, for the laſt ſix months, as Under Secretary of State in the American department, and to all the clerks who have been deprived of their ſituations in thoſe offices by their ſuppreſſion, acquainting them, that the Lords Commiſſioners of the Treaſury had made them all allowances in compenſation of the incomes they had been deprived of; and no ſuch letter having come to me, I am conſtrained to give you the trouble of this letter, to requeſt the favour of you to move their Lordſhips to permit you to inform me on what account it is that I, who had ſerved as Under Secretary to every Secretary of State that has filled the American department, from its inſtitution to its ſuppreſſion, and even attended the Earl of Shelburne when that department was abſorbed in the domeſtic, until his Lordſhip was more ably ſerved, ſhould be the only perſon paſſed over upon this occaſion

occasion without compensation, and even without notice.

"I am, Sir, &c.
"William Knox.
"Geo. Rose, Esq."

Copy of Mr. Rose's Answer, dated 17th of March 1783.

"Sir,

"Upon reading to my Lords Commissioners of the Treasury your letter, dated the 5th instant, respecting a compensation for your office of Under Secretary of State for the American department, I am directed to acquaint you, that my Lords are of opinion that you have no claim whatever to a compensation for the loss of your office, you having already a pension of six hundred pounds a-year for yourself, and the like sum for Mrs. Knox.

"I am, Sir, &c.
"Geo. Rose."

CHAPTER XXII.

LORD GEORGE GERMAIN.

Public Prejudice. His Conduct in early Life, and Character. Behaviour at Fontenoy. His Quarrel with Prince Ferdinand. His Conduct at Minden. Observations upon it. Antient Virtue. Modern Indifference. Commencement of the American War. Letter of the late Sir Joseph Yates. Answer to it. Lord George Germain appointed Secretary of State. Management of the London Gazette. Surrender of Lord Cornwallis. Disagreement in the Ministry. The Misfortune of Lord Cornwallis imputed to Lord Sandwich, and to Lord George Germain. This Disagreement appears in Parliament. Conduct of Mr. Dundas and Mr. Rigby. Application to Sir Guy Carleton. Substance of his Letter to the Lord Chancellor. Meeting of the Secret

Secret Cabinet. Lord George Germain removed.

AN unfavourable opinion, haftily adopted, was formed of the character of this noble Lord, from his conduct at the battle of Minden; and, like moſt precipitate opinions of character, was not wholly juſt, for whatever reprehenſion his conduct on that day might deſerve, it ought not to extend to every other circumſtance of his life.

At an early age he ſhewed himſelf worthy of his anceſtors. Nature had been to *him* a generous, a partial parent: ſhe had equally beſtowed her ſtriking ornaments on his external form, and on his mind. To a graceful perſon, and to an agreeable, manly, and expreſſive aſpect, ſhe had joined an accurate judgment, acuteneſs of thought, and elegance of imagination. Without theſe properties, in ſome degree, learning and manner, however elaborately impreſſed on the body and on the intellect, produce but cold effects.

During his youth, he became converſant with the manners of the court. There he ſoon acquired that inſtantaneous politeneſs, that habitual caſe and flexibility of behaviour, which, within the limits of ſtrict moral honour, improve and refine the man. But to deceive and to betray, thoſe barbarous arts which are daily taught, and conſummately practiſed in the circle of a court, he never would adopt.

This encomium is not taken from vague report; nor is it the language of adulation. It is the opinion of officers who ſerved under him, and who were his intimate acquaintance. The picture of him which they drew did much honour to the original. They have affirmed, that in his behaviour as a man, and in his deportment as a commander, dignity was moſt happily tempered with caſe, and the ſtrictneſs of military diſcipline with mildneſs and affability;—that he was a moſt inſtructive and engaging companion, a moſt faithful and zealous friend, and a moſt humane protector of his dependents. And from whom are we
to

to expect, rather than from those by whom he was thus represented, a true account of his social qualities? He has been accused of pride and haughtiness, but the charge is more invidious than true. As from great abilities naturally proceeds an energy of existence, they are generally attended with at least a temperate majesty of manner, and elocution, which may be very remote from pride; the sordid vice that commonly occupies a frivolous or a stupid mind. Besides, as it is the peculiar property of pride to hurt and disgust, and as vigorous and fine talents are sure to hurt and disgust understandings of a low class, the undistinguishing pigmies confound ideas, and as they are alike affected by pride and genius, they mistake both for the same object. There are likewise pressing junctures, in which the truly great man will break through the established forms, the polite moderation of the world, and ardently assert his natural and inalienable prerogatives. He will repel impertinence or insolence with an air and eloquence that petrify, with a lightning that withers his aggressor. The puny soul shrinks back into its little dark cell, appalled and confounded.

founded. No wonder if, ever after, it attributes the juſt and ſpirited reproof to habitual pride, that immoral and deſpicable quality. It would be impoſſible for a man of extraordinary mental endowments, to atone to the vulgar of the human race for his incommunicable pre-eminence, without ſinking to a timid and abject behaviour. Moſt exorbitant are the demands of dull, vain, and ſelfiſh mortals. They are for inverting the order of the intellectual creation, and would have us cringe to *them*. But certainly the lines in which our ſpecies is diſtinguiſhed by Ovid from the other animals, may be applied, with a ſingular propriety and emphaſis, to the man of tranſcendent capacity—

> Os Homini ſublime dedit, cœlumque tueri
> Juſſit, et erectos ad Sidera tollere vultus.

At the battle of Fontenoy, which was fought in the year 1744, he was wounded by a muſquet-ball. The wound was accidental, and only affected his body. His collected and manly behaviour, on that memorable day, was courage and principle. And it is well known that in his duel with Governor Johnſtone

stone (the particulars of which the reader will see in the Appendix, marked N.) he acquitted himself with a firmness and spirit which were never excelled on a similar occasion. From these facts no doubts can be entertained of his personal courage.

In the affair of Minden, it is not proper to view him with a prejudiced or an indulgent eye, but with impartial and accurate observation. And the appeal is made to those whose habitual and uniform benevolence is not merely the consequence of an ingenuous nature, but likewise of expanded thought and reflection; to those whose active and spirited candour flows from an enlarged and comprehensive knowledge of mankind; who in analysing the conduct of a man, never forget that the generous virtues are connected with strong passions; and that though there have been many bright characters, there was never one immaculate. No honest man can hesitate to pronounce him faulty. He ought to have advanced with the British horse, to complete the rout of the French infantry; he was not restrained from advancing by fear, but

but by a *perſonal reſentment*. He had not been properly reſpected by the commander of the allied army; and he had *determined*, when opportunity ſhould offer, to check the luxuriant growth of Prince Ferdinand's laurels. Phlegm, ſullenneſs, inhumanity, and a moſt inordinate love of power, are the characteriſtics of a German mind. He only delights in riot and homicide, like his Thracian god, Mars, to whom he ſacrifices many human victims, and to whom he pours many profuſe libations. As Prince Ferdinand's ideas were confined to the Gothic ſyſtem, he felt not, he knew not what reſpect was due to a ſon of one of the firſt families in England, and to a ſoldier adorned with the arts of the milder Minerva. He was likewiſe exaſperated againſt Lord George Sackville, who had counteracted the rapacity of this commander in chief, and had oppoſed his meaſures in councils of war, whenever he thought them injudicious. It is not neceſſary here to enter into a ſcrutiny of Prince Ferdinand's conduct; but it may be obſerved, that officers have ſaid that he owed his military fame far more to fortune than to prudence,

and

and a confummate, knowledge in the art of war. Indeed in every department of life, it is not fo much our merit as our fuccefs that gains us applaufe.

His free fentiments on the plans and operations of the campaign, and his watchful and penetrating infpection into military avarice, necefsarily brought on him the extreme hatred of the commander in chief; who therefore was induftrious to deprive him of that efteem and deference to which he was well entitled from the army. And if Lord George, with a fufceptible conftitution, and confcious of his natural and acquired fuperiority, as a man, over a high-rated myrmidon, retaliated the malice of the petty Prince with a permanent and keen difguft; the circumftance fhews, that it is poffible a man not wanting in courage, may fuffer his private paffion to influence his public duty. Such differences have frequently happened in every fervice, between great officers; and have as frequently been highly injurious to the public intereft. It ought to be in the penetration of a minifter to difcover thefe differences;

and

and whenever they happen, he should always withdraw one of the parties.

The keenness of irritation and the smart of insult may offer some apology to the generous heart and the enlightened mind, though it cannot excuse the fault. Passion is constitutional; but it is better that a character should be shaded by a warm and vigorous feeling, than by one that is cold and pusillanimous. It must give more pleasure to an Englishman to find, that it was resentment, not cowardice, that suspended the march of the cavalry in the plains of Minden.

If we review the lives of eminent men in private and public station; whose actions, on the whole, were good or great; we shall meet with some palpable offences against moral rectitude, and perhaps some crimes. In the virtuous times of those illustrious republics, Carthage and Rome, both the states were injured by the private animosities of some senators and commanders, who, notwithstanding, had many excellent qualities, and did signal services to their respective countries.

A truly

A truly wife man will dignify his life with fobriety, diligence, and integrity, whether he be in a public or private capacity, for his own fake; to fecure thofe ineftimable rewards, which are the confequences of virtue. But to fay that an Englifhman ought to toil or bleed for every fyftem of politics that a minifter thinks proper to adopt, is almoft the rant of infanity. Corruption, both public and private, is in its zenith; yet we talk as if we lived in an antient and fimple commonwealth, whofe wants were limited by nature; where every paffion was cool, except ardour for the public good; where that ardour was earneftly inculcated by precept, and emphatically enforced by ftriking examples; and where it confequently animated every member of the ftate. We talk as if we lived in Old Rome (long before fhe was decorated with her glaring magnificence); but when fhe had rifen to the fummit of real grandeur; when Curius boiled his turnips at his Sabine farm; when Cincinnatus held his plough; and when a hoftile king could neither frighten Fabricius with the new fight of his elephant, nor allure him with his gold.

It is this deception of ourselves that has brought us into so many difficulties. An attention to what we affect, and a regard to what we owe to ourselves, and to posterity, might have prevented many evils. The American war was unnecessary, unjust, and unprovoked. It is impossible the people of this country could have been duped into an approbation of that war, if they had given a proper attention to the measure at the beginning; but that blind confidence to which they have habituated themselves, gives opportunity and facility to any minister to exercise a despotic authority, wherever he pleases.

The American colonies had attained the full vigour of manhood. They considered themselves as bound to us by the indissoluble ties of common origin, of common names, common language, religion, and interest; and there subsisted between us and them the happiest reciprocation of wealth, affection, and power.

In the year 1775 the British nation was precipitated into a war with these colonies;
the

the caufes of which have been already related in Chapter xviii. under the head of Mr. Grenville. From this war, as from the womb of the Trojan horfe, have iffued a thoufand calamities. It has been pregnant with difafters to all Europe; nor is it yet known what may be the extent of its effects.

Lord George Germain was one of thofe members of parliament who approved of this war at the commencement of it; he had adopted all thofe opinions which were hoftile to America. He conceived that Great Britain had a right to lay taxes on America. He implicitly imbibed the whole extent of Mr. Grenville's opinions and principles. This was fo perfectly agreeable to the fecret and confidential cabinet of the court, that immediately after hoftilities had been commenced againft America, he was put at the head of the American department, and official fpies were placed about him to betray his meafures, and by every art and falfehood were ufed to confirm him in his opinions. Thefe fpies were the confidants of the fecret cabinet; and were placed in every office to give information of every thing that was tranfacting there, to fuggeft meafures, to lay down plans, and to alter them at the pleafure of the fecret, unrefponfible, and unconftitutional minifters.

An opinion has prevailed, that his adoption of Mr. Grenville's ideas and principles refpecting America, was in no fmall degree influenced by a letter written by the late Sir Jofeph Yates, one of the Judges of the Court of King's Bench, upon this fubject. If it be true, that fuch letter was a primary caufe of fo much mifchief, it is an hiftorical curiofity; and will pleafe all thofe perfons who have been of opinion that Great Britain had a *right* to tax America. The following is a copy of it:

Copy of a Letter from the late Sir Jofeph Yates, *to* Chriftopher Griffith, *Efq. Member for* Berks, *relative to the Difpute between* Great Britain *and her Colonies.*

" The American colonies are the fubject of every converfation—well may it be fo, for the crifis is very alarming.

" How

"How far the taxation was prudent or unseasonable, or whether the rates would be too high or not, I will not take upon me to form any judgment; but the right to tax them is so clear and self-evident, that I am astonished there should be any doubt about it; those who doubt, contend that no tax can be imposed without the consent of the people by their representatives; that the Americans have no representation in parliament, &c.

"But the true constitution is, That no money can be levied by the crown without the consent of the great council of the realm, that is, the parliament. To that council the rights of the subjects are entrusted as the barrier between the crown and the people: a barrier against the strides of prerogative, which, in the reign of King John, were enormous till his abitrary laws were restrained by Magna Charta. By that charter it is ordained, that no talliage or aid shall be imposed but by the common council of the realm; in that body, the will of the whole people is reposed by the constitution; they are

are the ftated guardians of the rights and liberties of the fubject; the platform that was laid when the conftitution was framed, and to which all our anceftors affented. To talk of perfonal reprefentation of every individual is abfurd; for ftrictly fpeaking, no man is the perfonal reprefentative of another, but who is actually chofen, and deputed by the perfon reprefented.

" But how many millions are there in this kingdom who have not a vote for a member of parliament, and yet are as liable to be taxed as the largeft freeholder? The truth is, that every fubject of the Britifh dominions, in whatever latitude the territory may be, is equally fubject to the Britifh legiflature fo long as he refides upon the territories, and enjoys the protection of the Englifh government; he owes an allegiance and fubmiffion to its laws; and whatever the nature of thofe laws may be, if the legiflature enact them, they are equally obligatory. Were it left to the Americans to diftinguifh between laws, and to defire what fort they would fubmit to, and what they would reject, there would soon be an end of all their subjection.

" The consent of parliament gives an equal sanction to all kinds of laws; and the same consent that is necessary to a money-bill, is necessary to any other law. And it is admitted, that all acts of parliament for the regulation of trade in the colonies, are binding upon them. In short, if the Americans are subjects at all, they are subjects to the laws and sovereignty of their mother country: and to controvert that power, to deny the obligation of its laws, is hardly consistent with subjection. And where is the injustice of taxing the Americans? Where protection is given, a tribute is due; and those who enjoy the benefit of a government, owe their share and contribution to the expences of maintaining it.

" The Americans are allowed all the rights and privileges of an English subject; they are entitled to inherit any possessions here, and have their properties at home protected by our laws: why then should they be exempt from the common burden of every subject; especially from those expences which their own protection occasions?

"I have given you a sketch of my own sentiments in this matter, because I imagined it is a topic in the country, as well as in town.

"Thursday, Jan. 30, 1763. J. Y."

There are a few words in one of Lord Chatham's speeches, which contain a full answer to this opinion of the Judge.

"Taxation is no part of the governing or legislative power. The taxes are a voluntary gift and grant of the Commons alone. In legislation the three estates of the realm are alike concerned, but the concurrence of the Peers and the Crown to a tax, is only necessary to close with the form of a law. The gift and grant is of the Commons alone. In ancient days, the Crown, the Barons, and the Clergy, possessed the lands. In those days, the Barons and the Clergy gave and granted to the Crown. They gave and granted what was

was their own. At present, since the discovery of America, and other circumstances permitting, the Commons are become the proprietors of the land. The property of the Lords, compared with that of the Commons, is as a drop of water in the ocean; and this House represents those Commons, the proprietors of the lands; and those proprietors virtually represent the rest of the inhabitants. When, therefore, in this House we give and grant, we give and grant what is our own. But in an American tax, what do we do? We, your Majesty's Commons for Great Britain, give and grant to your Majesty, what? Our own property?—No. We give and grant to your Majesty the property of your Majesty's Commons of America. It is an absurdity in terms."

Lord George Germain having supported Lord North in the bills for altering the government of Massachusett's Bay, and shutting up the port of Boston, was appointed Secretary of State for the American department; by which the conduct of the war against America was, in a great degree, put into his hands.

This was not a fituation, at the time it was undertaken, for caution and timidity; for the chicane of a Mazarine, or the chimera of a Duke of Orleans; but for the bold and decided policy of a Richlieu and a De Retz.

How his Lordfhip fucceeded in his new fituation, it is not the defign of this work to relate. The circumftances of the American war are in general pretty well known.

There was a paper afcribed to Richard Burke, Efq. (brother to Edmund Burke, Efq.) on the fubject of managing the London Gazette, at leaft it was fo intitled, in printing the accounts from America during the war, that was much taken notice of; and as it fhews that thofe accounts are not to be depended upon, the reader will not be difpleafed to fee it preferved. It is in the Appendix, marked O.

After waging war with America, by fea and land, from the beginning of April 1775, to the month of April 1782, at an immenfe expence

expence of blood and treasure, the court, and people of Great Britain, discovered that the continuation of the war was impracticable.

Two fine armies had been captured, and more men could not be obtained.

When the intelligence arrived in London, that Lord Cornwallis and his army had surrendered, the ministry immediately quarrelled amongst themselves. They laid the cause of this disaster upon each other; but at length they settled it upon only two persons: these were Lord Sandwich, and Lord George Germain. And it was resolved, that one of these must go out.

Those who laid the blame upon Lord Sandwich, contended, that the misfortune was owing to the not having a sufficient naval force on the American station.

Those who laid the blame upon Lord Germain, contended, that the misfortune was owing to the plan of operations.

It is not neceffary to ftate the facts, upon which thefe two opinions were founded. They have been publifhed by Lord Cornwallis and Sir Henry Clinton, in vindication of themfelves.

The contention upon the queftion, whether the Secretary of State, or the Firft Lord of the Admiralty, fhould be removed, lafted fome time.

In this divided ftate of the miniftry, parliament met; and on the firft day of the feffion it was obvious to every one, that the difpute was not fettled. In the debate on the addrefs, Lord George Germain faid, " That his opinion was, notwithftanding the furrender of Lord Cornwallis, that if Great Britain gave up the fovereignty of America, we were undone." Mr. Dundas, Lord Advocate of Scotland, contradicted, and reprobated this opinion feverely; and Mr. Rigby, who was Pay-mafter, bluntly faid, " We were beaten, and therefore muft give up the plan of the war." When parliament adjourned for the Chriftmas holidays, the difpute continued open.

It

It is certain, that when Lord George Germain delivered his opinion, he thought he delivered the opinion of a much greater authority than his own. But he was not entrusted with the *real secret*. There were other persons who were honoured with a larger share of confidence than he was at this time: and this party triumphed. They resolved to remove Lord George Germain from office; and to recall Sir Henry Clinton from America, who had requested it; and to make one measure the consequence of the other, although there was no connection between the two cases; but in order to make a connection between them, they applied to Sir Guy Carleton to succeed Sir Henry Clinton; they were perfectly well assured, that Sir Guy Carleton would not go to America, while Lord George Germain continued Secretary of State for the American department. The manœuvre succeeded. Sir Guy Carleton wrote a letter to the Lord Chancellor, (Lord Thurlow,) saying, in substance, that he could not accept the command under the American Secretary. The Lord Chancellor carried this letter into the closet.

On Wednesday the 2d of January 1782, previous to the levee, there was a meeting of Lord Mansfield, Lord Hillsborough, Lord Stormont, Lord North, and Mr. Jenkinson, now Earl of Liverpool, at his Lordship's house in Parliament-street. At this meeting, it was finally decided to remove Lord George Germain.

When Lord George was informed that his fate was decided, he desired leave to resign, to avoid the disgrace of being turned out, which favour was allowed him; and to lighten his fall, he was created an English peer.

After hawking the office about for some time, Mr. Ellis, now Lord Mendip, was prevailed upon to accept it: and, to preserve an appearance of consistency, Sir Guy Carleton was appointed successor to Sir Henry Clinton.

CHAPTER XXIII.

DAVID HARTLEY, Esq.

His Tract intitled " Right of Appeal to Juries, in Causes of Excise, asserted." The Budget. Intended Prosecution of that Tract. His State of the Nation. Letters to his Constituents of Hull. Acquaintance with Dr. Franklin. Appointed Minister Plenipotentiary. His Tract on the French Revolution.

THIS gentleman has written several tracts, which have been held in great estimation. The first was intitled, " The Right of Appeal to Juries, in Causes of Excise, asserted." This tract was occasioned by the extension of the Excise laws to the makers of cyder and perry, in Lord Bute's administration, in the year 1763. The reader will not be displeased with the following extract from it.

" The argument of those who support the principle of the cyder-act may be stated thus:

Cyder

Cyder made for the confumption of each private family, ought, by all principles of equality, to pay some duty; but such a tax cannot be raifed by a conftitutional mode of excife;" [the difference between the conftitutional and unconftitutional mode he defines to be this, the former is limited to the trader, the latter is extended to every private houfe;] " therefore, we muft feek our remedy by a capitation on the cyder drinkers. Well then, we are to hope that this capitation will be levied in a conftitutional manner. Let us judge: the excifeman is to be armed with unlimited powers of fearch, from the barn without to the clofet within; with an alternative offered to each perfon thus vifited, of efcaping all this vexation upon a certain compofition for the duty. Now, becaufe there is an alternative offered, this is faid to be a law formed upon the principles of liberty; for no man is forced under this excife: the law only compels him under intolerable pains and penalties to a voluntary payment. I wifh fome clear-fighted man would explain to me the difference between thefe two cafes: the miniftry fend me notice, that I fhall have a troop of excife-men,

men, or a troop of horse, (no matter which,) quartered upon me; and in a postscript they subjoin, that a troop of horse is but (as the gentlemen of the long-robe say) a fiction in law; and if I will pay half-a-crown a-head for my family, I shall hear no more of the excisemen, or the troop of horse, till the next time. Another man (not so correct perhaps in his spelling) writes me word that he will set fire to my house, unless I deposit ten guineas under a certain tree. The argument of the ministry is, can you complain of a burden as intolerable, when we offer you so reasonable an alternative, as that of paying your half-crowns? My illiterate correspondent says, is not your house worth saving at so small a price as ten guineas? Shooting at you behind a hedge, or burning your house, are but fictions in law: pay your money quietly, and sleep in peace till it comes to your turn again. The principle in these two cases is the same; I wish their fates had not been different. The one is branded as it deserves in the black act; while the other stalks abroad in open and insolent defiance.

" It

"It is a grievance throughout the whole fyftem of the excife laws, that cafes of appeal at the fuit of the fubject, are not to be tried by juries. I fhall examine the merits of the queftion, of allowing an appeal to juries, upon the following topics: whether it will tend to the diminution of the revenue, in fuch excifes as only affect the trader; and whether it will not fpecifically apply a remedy to the intolerable grievances of an unconftitutional excife, and difappoint a farther extenfion of this horrid mode. As to the firft, it is faid, that in trials between the crown and fubject, juries will foon get into a habit of deciding againft the crown. To which I reply, that the revenue of the cuftoms bears a conftant teftimony againft this ftrange principle: for if this fuppofed infamous partiality of juries were fo notorioufly to be depended upon, why does not every man who has a duty of the cuftoms to pay, leave the matter to trial for the chance of evading it? Afk the lawyers who have pleaded for the crown, whether juries do not feel the force of their arguments, that every fraud committed to the detriment of the revenue, and connived at, is

an

an act of oppreffion and injuftice to the fair trader? There is no argument or experience to fix fo deteftable an imputation upon an Englifh jury. What intereft can a jury be fuppofed to have between the crown and a petty trader; a foap-boiler, for inftance, or a tallow-chandler? Are thefe the objects of popular adoration, againft whom no jury fhall give their profane verdict? If not, where is the danger to the revenue of excife, as confined to the trader and retailer, if juries be allowed? Why fhould the Minifter have power or influence to inflict any tax, (under the fevereft pains and penalties to be decided without appeal,) which no twelve jurymen in the kingdom fhall think confiftent with liberty? This is the touchftone of excife: will it endure an open appeal to juries? If it will, it is admiffible; if not, no.

" There are two kinds of excife, the one limited to the trader; the other, extended to the concerns of private and domeftic life. The appeal to juries in the one is expedient, in the other indifpenfable; as well to prevent

the

the encroachment, as to defeat the tyranny of a general excife."

His next tract was intitled " The Budget. Infcribed to the Man who thinks himfelf Minifter." For fome time, this tract was attributed to Sir George Savile, and the late Right Honourable Charles Townfhend, in his defence of the Minority, on the queftion relating to general warrants, gave currency to this opinion, for he faid in it, " That Lord Halifax might iffue out another general warrant under pretence of the laft libel the Budget; and he may order, as he did before, fix meffengers to inquire for the author, and to feize upon any perfon whom they think proper, and his papers; and what law remains in allowed force to deter them from feizing, upon the ground of received opinion, the perfon of that honourable gentleman, whom fome people allege they know, and many believe, to have been, in part at leaft, the author of that excellent and unanfwered work? In this cafe it is true, the outcry would be great and general, from the character of the perfon
thus

thus treated; his ancient family; his extensive, though concealed generosity, and his popularity in that large manufacturing and wealthy county, which he reprefents with fuch entire fatisfaction to his conftituents, and fo much reputation to himfelf." See the article in the Appendix marked P.

Perhaps Sir George Savile might give to Mr. Hartley fome affiftance, but the latter gentleman was undoubtedly the writer. The Budget was a very fharp attack upon Mr. Grenville's plan of finance for the year 1764. Mr. Grenville was very much hurt by it. There was a paragraph in it, near the end, upon which he intended to have inftituted a profecution. The paragraph was as follows:

" There is a degree of malice in the prefent miniftry, againft their country, that is beyond example. They forced themfelves by violence and intrigue into the conduct of public affairs, at a time when the general voice of their country was loudly againft them. They came in to expofe the pretended nakednefs of their country, to an enemy who was at the last gasp. They vilified our advantages; they falsified our situation; they proclaimed our distress in the most exaggerated terms, when that very distress, compared with the real calamities of our enemies, was triumph. Upon that fatal day, when this system of ministry came to the helm, was first promulgated the desolation and debility of this country. Instead of shewing to our enemies the hopelessness of their situation, they gave them encouragement to expect an universal confusion here; minister lying in wait to perplex minister; brother to supplant brother; and the whole system of affairs thrown into a treacherous consternation. Advertisements went to the enemy, that, if they would hold their breath a few hours, we would raise the clamour for peace here; instead of telling them, that we had at that moment the funds for two years to come, viz. the beer duty granted in December 1760, and the spirit duties, which had been granted the preceding session, but were postponed for the service of the year 1762; [and even Mr. Whately, in his Considerations on Trade and Finances, admits that

money

money to carry on the war, might, at that time, have been obtained at three per cent.] which at the pinch of the war, is the point gained; and, therefore, that they (the enemies), could have nothing to hope for, but still to be beaten for two complete years, by an enemy in the full career of victory. Neither could this prove a vain boaſt, for the faculties of this country were ſo far from being exhauſted, that, at that hour, we were provided with funds for more money than all our previous ſucceſſes had coſt us: inſomuch, that on the eighteenth of December 1760, the parliament having provided twelve millions for the next year, we had ſtill left another fund capable of producing twelve millions more, to be poſtponed for the ſervice of a farther year, being thus ſuperabundantly provided. In this height of glory did the evil genius of this country aim the fatal blow, which has reduced us to be faithleſs and friendleſs throughout the world."

Upon the preceding extract, the opinion of the Honourable Mr. Charles Yorke was taken; and he pronounced it to be a libel:

but Mr. Grenville consulted some of his friends, who thought differently from Mr. Yorke; and the opinion prevailing, that the Budget had been written by Sir George Savile, it was not judged prudent to commence a profecution againſt a character of ſuch eminence and refpectability.

In the year following, (1765,) Mr. Hartley wrote another tract on the fame fubject, which he called, "The State of the Nation; with a preliminary Defence of the Budget." This defence of the Budget was a reply to the tract intitled "Remarks on the Budget," which had been written under Mr. Grenville's eye, by Mr. Charles Lloyd, who was his private fecretary. The State of the Nation confifted of Mr. Hartley's account of the finances of that year.

At the commencement of the year 1768, he publiſhed another tract on the finances, which he intitled " A Caveat on the Part of Public Credit, previous to the opening of the Budget for the prefent Year 1768."

The

The celebrity of thefe tracts, and his general knowledge of finance, induced his friends to wifh to fee him in parliament.

He was accordingly elected for Kingfton upon Hull; but not until the American troubles had commenced. His conduct in Parliament was almoft confined to queftions and motions relating to thofe troubles. His conftant and moft anxious defire was a reconciliation between the mother country and her colonies. His frequent motions in parliament in order to obtain peace with America, and his arguments in fupport of thofe motions, are to be found in the Parliamentary Regifter of that time. But a tract which he publifhed, intitled " Letters on the American War; addreffed to the Mayor, Corporation, and Burgeffes of Hull;" contain his own ftatement of his conduct in parliament; together with many facts and arguments which are not any where elfe to be met with.

Thefe letters develope the caufes, and ftate the impolicy of the war with America, in a very ftrong and intelligent manner: and his

being

being the intimate friend of Dr. Franklin, Mr. Digges, and several other American gentlemen, during their residence in England, previous and until the commencement of the war, leaves no doubt that the several facts, deductions, and arguments, therein stated, are all of them well founded; and therefore are peculiarly interesting to the future inquirer. The impartial historian of this period, if ever such a person should arise, will receive an invaluable fund of materials from this gentleman's writings.

His thorough knowledge of the American subject, and his intimacy with Dr. Franklin, pointed him out as the most proper person to negotiate the treaty of peace with America, in the year 1783. He was accordingly appointed Minister Plenipotentiary to Paris, for that purpose, and concluded the treaty.

In the year 1794 he wrote another tract, which he intitled "Argument on the French Revolution, and the Means of Peace." In this tract, Mr. Hartley has stated the causes and importance of the French revolution, in the

clearest

cleareſt manner poſſible: an extract from it will therefore not be unacceptable to the reader.

"The French," he ſays, "fell into civil conteſts, a few years ago, reſpecting ſome propoſed reformations of their political conſtitution. In the period of three years, from 1789 to 1791, the reformations were completed, and the conſtitution renovated upon principles of reaſon and inveſtigation, with the aſſent of the then King and People of France. From a deſpotic it became a limited monarchy; all the intolerable grievances of deſpotiſm being expelled, and the new government reformed, as nearly as the caſe would admit, upon principles ſimilar to the limited monarchy of Great Britain.

"It does not appear that ſurrounding nations thought very deeply of the reſulting and influential example of deſpotiſm reformed within the bounds of reaſon and Britiſh liberties. The ſovereigns of Europe, blinded with faſtidious deſpotiſm, ſeemed to deſpiſe the

the influence of reason as unworthy of their regard. But when the systematic perseverance of three years had brought the great work into a practicable shape, they began to fear the influential example of reformed despotism, and from that period confederacies of European powers were formed for the destruction of the new constitution of France, and for the partition of its territory. The dates of these conventions and treaties were long before any hostile preparations on the part of France. The treaty of Pavia was on the 6th of July 1791; the convention of Pilnitz on the 26th of August 1791; and various other preparatory treaties, on the part of the sovereigns of Europe, were formed in the course of the year 1791. Of all these matters, explanations were demanded on the part of France, and refused by the combined powers; and (according to the customs of nations) France declared war upon the refusal of various necessary explanations—such as, the cause of armaments by the combined powers, the coalition with the French emigrants, supplying them with arms, &c. &c.

"All

" All these points are now become facts of notoriety.

" The French did not declare war with the Emperor until the month of April 1792, which was many months subsequent to various treaties and confederacies entered into against France by the Emperor, and most of the European powers. The forbearance on the part of France, considering the notoriety of various treaties against themselves, with the public and avowed support, inrolment, and arming of the emigrants, was very much within the ordinary forbearance of independent states, and in no degree to compare, for peremptory promptitude of defiance, to the proceedings of the British ministry, in the year 1756, in taking 25,000 seamen from the French, before the declaration of war. In the dubious state of alarm in which the National Assembly found themselves involved, in the beginning of the year 1792, it was undoubtedly not their interest to provoke hostilities with all surrounding nations. They were fully apprised of the hostile disposition of the European powers to their new constitution, and still more apprehensive of the insincerity of the French court itself, against the reformed constitution, although it had been accepted by the King, with the fullest professions of choice and complacence. The great object of jealousy, at that time was the Austrian Committee, so called; of the existence of which, the proofs or presumptions are not within our view, any farther than as they may argue, that the French were urged into the war, by confederacy of councils, as well as preparations of arms against them.

" I dwell upon the indisposition of the French to be involved in universal war, because it was so much their interest to have avoided it, in the beginning, and still more remains their interest now, to be extricated from war. From thence I draw this inference, that the French will be disposed, at any moment, to concur in the abatement of the war, on the condition of being left unmolested by other nations, respecting their new constitution; and on their parts leaving all other nations unmolested in all their dominions

minions and forms of government, and all other interests whatsoever.

"A very notorious proof occurred in the commencement of the revolution, to shew, that the new government of France neither had, nor could have, any interest in disturbing the governments of other countries, not even in a case where an obvious fraternity of cause seemed to call upon them. The States of Brabant, by their Plenipotentiary, M. Vandernoot, presented a letter of requisition to the Assembly and the King, requesting the interposition of the power of France, in support of their recent claims of emancipation from the dominion of the Emperor, their sovereign. But the National Assembly totally refused all aid and interference; they persisted, through the course of an whole twelvemonth, to remain tranquil and passive by-standers, whilst the Imperial power pursued and effected the complete re-conquest of the Austrian Flanders, by force of arms. This refusal to interfere in any civil contest, foreign to them, continued through the whole of the year 1790; but after the year 1791, when the Emperor Leopold

pold began to negotiate a general confederacy of the powers of Europe againſt the new conſtitution of France, the National Aſſembly took up, with rage, the cauſe of Belgic liberty, as an act of hoſtility to that prince, who had put himſelf at the head of the grand confederacy of ſovereigns, againſt the liberation of the commons of France. This act was therefore an act of defenſive hoſtility, after a previous declaration of war againſt the Emperor.

"Similar conduct ſtands in frequent example among nations. Henry IV. of France, and Queen Elizabeth of England, did both ſupport the original revolt of the Belgic provinces againſt Philip II. of Spain. Charles I. of England ſupported the proteſtant inſurgents at Rochelle, againſt the tyranny of the crown of France, during the adminiſtration of Cardinal Richlieu: but the power of Richlieu prevailed, and the French nation has groaned under the cruelties of deſpotiſm, from that fatal day, until the preſent revolution of liberty and rights. Louis XIV. and Louis XV. ſupported various rebellions againſt the decided conſtitutions of theſe kingdoms.

doms. 'Louis XVI. fupported the American caufe againft the claims of taxation and legiflation on the part of Great Britain.

" There is no device of war more ftudied, or more frequently put into practice, than exciting civil tumults in an enemy's country. If the French Convention had confined their decrees of revolutionary fraternization, fpecifically to nations with whom they were actually at war, or under fuch violent prefumption of meditated injury, as would have juftified a declaration, or an act of war, (according to the laws of nations,) no exception could have been taken to their conduct. But their declarations were general and unqualified, and therefore gave general and juftifiable offence. When the miniftry of Great Britain remonftrated againft the unqualified generality of fraternizing decrees, the French miniftry gave an explanation, which although it might not be confidered as the obvious conftruction upon the decree of November 19, 1792, was, however, a proferred explanation, and therefore might have been accepted as the *amende honorable*, reducing the principle of of revolutionary fraternization to the quali-, fied cafe, towards nations in hoftility. It was a moft unfortunate meafure, infinitely to be lamented, that the qualifying explanation was not accepted. If it had been accepted, all the miferies of war might have been faved, and we might have been at peace now. No nation is to be prefumed, from a lapfe of phrafe, fubfequently retracted, to remain in the perfevering intention of doing any act, not only contrary to their retractation, but, moft of all, contrary to their intereft.

" The French nation have given a full proof in the cafe of the Belgian revolution, that they are not ready to declare themfelves the univerfal champions of revolutionary liberty, throughout the world. There was great prudence of conduct in that reftraint. Neither has that prudence deferted them at this hour. In their new conftitution of June 1793, they have inferted, as a fundamental and declaratory principle, the political independence of nations. They fay, ' they will ' not interfere in the government of other ' nations; they will not fuffer other nations
' to

' to interfere with the government of their
' own.' (Article 119 of the *acte constitutionel*
of the French Republic, 1793.) I am anxious
to explain this point: becaufe it appears to
me to have been the only embarraffment to
the negotiation of peace. The article preceding that above-mentioned (viz. article
118) is very fignificant on this head of clear-
ing the way to negotiation of peace: viz.
article 118, ' The French people are the friend
' and natural ally of *free people*.' The peculiar view of this article is to exprefs, that fraternization does not commence except with
nations, either in poffeffion, or in the active
vindication of civil freedom, by the univerfal
and unequivocal exertion of the national will:
thereby fignifying that they do not offer their
fraternization to urge nations to the overthrow of any governments exifting in tranquillity, for the purpofe, even of political
emancipation, by the excitement of a civil
war. They have felt the offence which a
lapfe of precifion in phrafe has excited againft
them; and therefore they purfue the recovery
of that lapfe, by the peace-offering to all foreign nations, contained in thefe two articles.

" It

" It is not poffible that the French nation can have any other view than peace, and the poffeffion of their new conftitution.—The fubftance of this article, 118, is precifely the conftruction which M. Chauvelin offered to the British miniftry, in abatement of the offence which had been taken with the unqualified fraternizing decree of November 1792. If the confederate nations have any real defire for peace, confiftent with fecurity to themfelves, the purport of thefe overtures is moft evidently calculated to give them full fatisfaction. They are a peace-offering to thofe who are willing to underftand.

" We are furrounded in a world of confternation. Novel principles of fociety have now taken poffeffion of the minds of men throughout the world. The fcience of politics is no longer limited merely to the arrangement of a balance of powers between the various members of any community, as in a ftate of contentious fociety: the doctrine of free compact, founded on the Rights of Man, is now claimed by mankind in a mafs, as their indefeafible right. Twenty-five millions

lions of men have thrown down the gauntlet in that cause. By this principle the rights in society are now to be decided; the challenge is loudly proclaimed, and will not brook evasion or delay. I suspect the compulsive application of this principle is nearer to all despotic governments than is generally apprehended. We cannot but recognize a principle capable of that application, in recent events, which have already decided in one moment of time the total fate of the French revolution. A London Gazette, reciting the tumults of October 5 and 6, 1789, states, that ' the word to fire was no sooner given, than ' the *Regiment de Flandre* clubbed their arms ' to a man, and other regiments also laid ' down their arms.' An important secret is here developed; which is, that the multitudinous and inferior ranks of men, who stand in rank and file, have a decisive negative in all civil contests, by clubbing their arms to a man. The contest in France has been a civil war between two classes of men; the one class consisting of twenty-four millions, the other class of one million. The high, few; the many, low. From the highest pinnacle

VOL. II. M to

to the lowest abyss! A horrid chasm between! In this tremendous chasm has the despotism of France been ingulphed.—A sermon of deep instruction to mankind!

" There is another royal document that generalizes the foregoing. It bears the title of ' Reasons that his Prussian Majesty opposes ' to the general Armament of the Inhabitants ' of the Empire of Germany,' *viz.* (after some previous, but not unimportant matter)

' That it is infinitely dangerous at a time ' like the present, when the French are watch- ' ing every advantage to insinuate their prin- ' ciples, to assemble such a mass of men, ' whose ideas upon forms of government ' must be various, and amongst whom, con- ' sequently, dissensions might arise, disastrous ' in their consequences both to the armies and ' to the constitution of the empire.'

" This declaration baffles all comment, and defies all aggravation. The whole empire of Germany is declared to be on the tiptoe of insurrection, congenial in sentiment, and pre-
meditating

meditating in their hearts to follow the example of France. All the expecting millions of the German empire are thus superadded to the actual millions of revolutionists in France. And if these are truths respecting the nations of Germany and France, it follows, by inevitable consequence, that all other millions throughout *despotic* nations of Europe are in a state of preparation and promptitude to receive those principles of resistance to despotism, which the French are watching every advantage to insinuate. The arguments in this manifesto have no bounds; they generalize the principles of the French revolution, to the predestinated destruction of every *despotic* government throughout the world."

CHAPTER XXIV.

JOSIAH WEDGWOOD, Esq.

His Discoveries, Taste, and Merits as a Manufacturer: as a Philosopher: as an inland Navigator. His institution of an Association in London, which he called the General Chamber of Manufacturers of Great Britain. His Opposition to Mr. Pitt's Propositions concerning the Trade with Ireland. Account of the Chamber of Manufacturers. The Members of the Chamber differ on the Commercial Treaty with France. The Chamber dissolved.

HE was the maker of his own fortune; and his country has been benefited by his exertions in a proportion not to be calculated.

His many discoveries of new species of earthen wares and porcelains, his studied forms and chaste style of decoration, and the correctness and judgment with which all his works

works were executed under his own eye, and by artifts for the moſt part of his own forming, have turned the current in this branch of commerce; for, before his time, England imported the finer earthen wares, but for more than twenty years paſt he has exported them to a very great annual amount, the whole of which is drawn from the earth; and from the induſtry of the inhabitants; while the national taſte has been improved, and its reputation raiſed in foreign countries.

His inventions have prodigiouſly increaſed the number of perſons employed in the potteries, and in the traffic and tranſport of their materials from diſtant parts of the kingdom; and this claſs of manufactures is alſo indebted to him for much mechanical contrivance and arrangement in their operations; his private manufactory having had for thirty years and upwards, all the efficacy of a public work of experiment.

Neither was he unknown in the walks of philoſophy—His communications to the Royal Society,

Society, of which he was a member, shewed a mind enlightened by science, and contributed to procure him the esteem of scientific men at home, and throughout Europe.

At an early period of his life, seeing the impossibility of extending considerably the manufactory he was engaged in, on the spot which gave him birth, without the advantages of inland navigation, he was the proposer of the Grand Trunk Canal, and the chief agent in obtaining the act of parliament for making it, against the prejudices of the landed interest, which at that time stood very high, and but just before had been with great difficulty overcome in another quarter by all the powerful influence of a noble Duke, whose canal was at that time the only one that had been constructed in this kingdom. The Grand Trunk Canal is ninety miles in length, uniting the rivers Trent and Mersey; and branches have since been made from it to the Severn, to Oxford, and to many other parts, and it will also have a communication with the Grand Junction Canal from Braunston to Brentford.

He was the founder, and chief promoter, of an affociation of manufacturers in London, which he denominated " The General Chamber of the Manufacturers of Great Britain."

The occafion of this inftitution was, Mr. Pitt's propofitions, in the year 1786, for adjufting the commercial intercourfe between Great Britain and Ireland.

When thefe propofitions were made public, Mr. Wedgwood faw them pregnant with infinite mifchiefs to the Britifh manufacturers: with many he converfed, and to others he wrote. He was active and affiduous in writing and printing, upon this great national fubject. He circulated his opinions in handbills, in letters, effays, and paragraphs, in the newfpapers; and by every poffible mode that he could take, to alarm the manufacturers of the whole kingdom; and direct their attention to the feveral fubjects, and parts of the propofitions which affected their particular interefts. Under a leader of fuch penetration and induftry, the affociation was quickly formed, of all the principal manufacturers, who, by either perfonal attendance, or by delegates, became members of it.

Thomas Walker, Efq. of Manchefter, was, next to Mr. Wedgwood, the moft ardent and active member. His account of the General Chamber of Manufacturers is worthy of notice.

With refpect to the origin of the Chamber, he fays, every one knew the occafion of its being inftituted at the time it was; and muft be fenfible, that it was intended to give that union and ftrength to the manufacturing interefts of Great Britain, which they had never before obtained, and which they never ftood more in need of than at that period—to arreft the hand then lifted up to give a moft deep and dangerous wound to the manufactures of this kingdom. He alluded to the propofitions fent from the Irifh to the Britifh Parliament, for its affent.

When the alarm had taken place to a confiderable degree, it was obferved with concern, how little effect was produced by appli-

applications from single and unconnected individuals. Their voice was too feeble to be heard alone. A meeting was therefore proposed, and held, of manufacturers in London, and such delegates and individuals from the country as were then in town, to consider of their situation, as well as that of the British manufacturers at large, and the steps necessary to be taken, both for their present safety and future protection. The resolutions entered into at that and the subsequent meetings were laid before the public.

Thus did the General Chamber of Manufacturers of Great Britain originate from the too well founded apprehensions of imminent danger to some of their most essential interests as manufacturers; and not from any party or factious motives, as had been falsely asserted by some, and too easily believed by others.

One circumstance he could not omit, as it exhibited a spirit of true patriotism in the gentlemen who composed the Chamber, and a confidence in the honour and integrity of their brethren, which did the highest credit

both

both to the one and to the other. The Chamber (he afferted, he fpoke from his own perfonal knowledge) finding, that in the bufinefs before them, there was not a moment to be loft, nobly difdained to wafte any time, or a fingle thought, upon pecuniary matters, which might be adjufted afterwards at greater leifure; but advanced, without hefitation, the money neceffary for all immediate calls, and pledged themfelves for the reft. This, he faid, was an inftance of that unbounded confidence which, when occafion calls for it, one honeft member of a community ought to place in another; and this confidence would be continued among members of any fociety, fo long as there remained fufficient virtue to deferve it. And whilft this confidence was preferved and kept up between the body of Manufacturers and their General Chamber, it would be the fureft pledge to them of protection againft any future intended blow, which might be too fudden in its approach to admit of otherwife collecting the fcattered ftrength of the manufacturers to withftand it, and too weighty in its nature for any fingle arm to defend itfelf againft.

With

With regard to the effects of the measures which had been taken from time to time by the members of the Chamber, it would require much detail to bring them forward to public view; but one of the principal ought by no means to pass unnoticed.—When, to their utter astonishment, they were first informed, from undoubted authority, that the Irish propositions must neither be altered nor modified in any respect whatever, but must stand or fall precisely in their original form; they immediately sent a deputation to rhe Minister to pray for time, if it was even but for a few days, till they could consult their constituents in the country; and upon receiving an absolute refusal, together with a confirmation of the above from the Minister himself, and a declaration, at the same time, that the business should be brought on in the House of Commons, in two days at farthest—a petition was immediately drawn up, signed, and presented the next day to the House, praying, that the petitioners might be heard by themselves and counsel, against the propositions.——It was by this judicious and well-timed measure that the ruin attendant upon the Irish propositions was first averted; and it was to the subsequent spirited and unwearied exertions of the Chamber, together with the support they received from the friends of our manufactures in both Houses of Parliament, that we owe the alterations which the propositions underwent, and the change of the original *eleven* into *twenty*; which, by procuring *time for due consideration,* caused the ultimate disgust conceived against the *whole,* by the most respectable and independent part of Parliament, and by almost, if not the whole, of the people of Ireland.

If, at that important crisis, there had not been a body ready to act with that promptness and resolution which the occasion demanded, if the manufacturers throughout the island must first have been consulted, the opportunity, so happily seized, would have been lost for ever, and the consequences in all probability would have been fatal to our best interests. The original propositions would, most probably, have been, at this day, the established law of the land; and many

many British manufacturers would have felt the ruinous effects of that law, before they became acquainted with its nature, or mode of operation. How many other important matters may yearly arise, and call for the like promptness both in decision and execution, the wisest man could not foresee: and if this institution, even in its infant and unsupported state, (rendered also, by the complexion of affairs at that time, so obnoxious to the Treasury Bench, that it was determined it should, if possible, be crushed,) if, in that situation, it had rendered us such essential services, what might we not expect from its riper years, when government should be convinced of its integrity and impartiality, and place confidence in its informations——when it should be guided, patronized, and supported by the wisdom and counsel, as well as by the purses, of the principal and most experienced manufacturers throughout Great Britain?

The project intended by the Irish propositions being totally defeated, the members of the Chamber held their meetings only occasionally.

casionally. But in the following year, 1787, an event happened which called forth all their active exertions. This was the commercial treaty with France, negotiated by Mr. Eden, now Lord Auckland. Upon this subject, Mr. Wedgwood was as ardent in support of Mr. Pitt, as he had before been against him. And Mr. Walker, viewing the commercial treaty in a very different light from Mr. Wedgwood, the Chamber became divided. Mr. Wedgwood, and those who were of his opinion, absented themselves; and in a little time the Association was dissolved. A few copies of the proceedings of the Chamber, concerning the treaty with France, were printed, but not published. As it is possible that in some future day they may be useful, the reader will see them preserved in the Appendix, marked Q.

CHAPTER XXV.

DR. BENJAMIN FRANKLIN.

Founder of American Greatness. Bred at Boston. Printer at Philadelphia. Comes to London. Returns to America. Made Clerk of the Assembly, and Post-Master of Philadelphia. Proposes, with Success, an Association to defend the Province. Elected a Member of the General Assembly. Disputes between the Proprietaries and the Assembly. The Answers to the Governor's Messages, ascribed to Dr. Franklin. Quotation from one of them. Made Post-Master-General of all America. Proposes the Congress held at Albany. Plan of the Albany Union. Another Plan proposed, and communicated to Dr. Franklin. His Answers to it. Northern Frontier attacked: levies Troops, and goes to protect it. Sent Agent to England. Settles the Disputes between the Proprietaries and the Assembly. Honours conferred on him in Great Britain. Answers a Pamphlet written by Messieurs Burkes. Returns to America. Receives the Thanks of the Assembly,

Assembly, and rewarded for his Services. Appointed Agent again. His Conduct on this Occasion well known. Visits the Continent of Europe. Petitions, with others, for a Grant of Lands on the Ohio. Report of the Board of Trade against the Petition. Dr. Franklin's Answer to the Report of the Board of Trade. Prayer of the Petition granted. Lord Hillsborough resigns on that Account. Affair of Hutchinson's and Oliver's Letters. Dr. Franklin leaves England. War with America. Appointed Minister Plenipotentiary to France. His Conductors removed from the Queen's House. Orrery destroyed in America. War should not be made on the Sciences. Several Attempts to open a Negotiation with him at Paris. His Friendship for Mr. Silas Deane. Sends Mr. Thornton to England. Instance of Mr. Fox's great political Sagacity. Dr. Franklin concludes the Peace between Great Britain and America. He returns to America. His Philosophy. Dies. Honours to his Memory.

OF this Philosopher, Legislator, and Statesman, it will be said, that like the Czar, Peter the First, he was the projector and founder of his country's greatnefs and power. He wifhed moft fincerely for the continuance of the connection between Great Britain and her colonies; becaufe he was convinced, it was the mutual intereft of both to preferve it. But when he faw the councils of Great Britain violently proceeding to the point of enflaving America, he devoted the force of his underftanding and penetration to the Intereft of his country.

He was bred a printer at Bofton in New England. At the age of only feventeen years, he quitted his father at Bofton, and went to Philadelphia, where he followed his profeffion fome time. His talents foon diftinguifhed him. He was encouraged to go to London to perfect himfelf in the knowledge of his trade. He remained in London feveral years; after which he returned to Philadelphia, and commenced trade on his own account, as a printer and ftationer, and met with the greateft fuccefs.

In the year 1736 he was appointed clerk to the General Affembly of Pennfylvania, and poft-mafter of the city of Philadelphia.

In the year 1744, during the war between Great Britain and France, some French and Indians committed several depredations on the frontier inhabitants of the province, who were entirely defenceless. At this crisis Franklin stepped forth, and proposed to a meeting of the citizens of Philadelphia, a plan of association, for the defence of the province. This was approved of, and signed by twelve hundred persons immediately; and in a few days the number of signers amounted to ten thousand. Franklin was chosen colonel of the Philadelphia regiment.

In the year 1747 he was chosen representative for Philadelphia, in the General Assembly of Pennsylvania. Warm disputes at this time subsisted between the Assembly and the proprietaries; each contending for what they conceived to be their rights. Franklin, a friend to the rights of man from his infancy, soon distinguished himself as an opponent to the schemes of the proprietaries. He was looked up to as the head of the opposition; and to him have been attributed many of the replies of the assemblies, to the

messages

messages of the governors. His manner was plain and mild: his style of speaking was, like that of his writing, simple, unadorned, and concise. With this plain manner, and his penetrating and solid judgment, he was able to confound the most eloquent and subtile of his adversaries. In one of the answers of the assembly to the governor, there is a short passage of great beauty and sublimity. It is in these words; "Those who would give up essential liberty, to purchase a little temporary safety, deserve neither liberty nor safety." Upon which, the writer of the Historical Review of Pennsylvania makes this remark, "There is not in any volume, the sacred writings excepted, a passage to be found better worth the veneration of free men." Page 290. edit. 1759.

In the year 1753, Dr. Franklin having conducted himself so well in the office of postmaster for Philadelphia, was appointed postmaster general for all America.

In the year 1754, when the French in Canada had made several encroachments on the back settlements of the British colonies, and greatly interrupted their trade with the Indians, the measure of a general congress was suggested by Dr. Franklin, to consist of commissioners from the different colonies. The idea was approved. The commissioners were appointed, and met at Albany in the month of July 1754, to form a plan of union for their common defence.

The plan they agreed upon was, in short, this: " That a grand council should be formed, of members to be chosen by the assemblies and sent from all the colonies; which council, together with a governor general to be appointed by the crown, should be empowered to make general laws to raise money in all the colonies for the defence of the whole." This plan was sent to the government in England for approbation. America thought herself sufficiently able to cope with the French, without other assistance; several of the colonies having alone in former wars withstood the whole power of the enemy, unassisted not only by the mother country, but by any of the neighbouring provinces. The plan, however,

ever, was not approved in England; but a new one was formed instead of it; by which it was proposed, that " the governors of all the colonies, attended by one or two members of their respective councils, should assemble, concert measures for the defence of the whole, erect forts where they judged proper, and raise what troops they thought necessary, with power to draw on the treasury in England for the sums that should be wanted; and the treasury to be reimbursed by a tax laid on the colonies by act of parliament."

This new plan being communicated by Governor Shirley to Dr. Franklin, occasioned the following letters from Dr. Franklin; which are worthy of preservation, as historical documents:

" Sir, Tuesday morning.
" I return the loose sheets of the plan, with thanks, to your Excellency for communicating them.

" I apprehend, that excluding the *people* of the colonies from all share in the choice of the Grand Council, will give extreme dissatisfaction, as well as the taxing them by act of parliament, where they have no representative. It is very possible, that this general government might be as well and faithfully administered without the people, as with them; but where heavy burdens have been laid on them, it has been found useful to make it, as much as possible, their own act; for they bear better when they have, or think they have, some share in the direction; and when any public measures are generally grievous or even distasteful to the people, the wheels of government must move more heavily."

"SIR,   Wednesday morning.

" I mentioned it yesterday to your Excellency as my opinion, that excluding the *people* of the colonies from all share in the choice of the Grand Council, would probably give extreme dissatisfaction, as well as the taxing them by act of parliament, where they have no representative. In matters of general concern to the people, and especially where burdens are to be laid upon them, it is of use to
consider,

consider, as well what they will be apt to think and say, as what they ought to think: I shall, therefore, as your Excellency requires it of me, briefly mention what of either kind occurs to me on this occasion.

" First, they will say, and perhaps with justice, that the body of the people in the colonies are as loyal, and as firmly attached to the present constitution, and reigning family, as any subjects in the king's dominions.

" That there is no reason to doubt the readiness and willingness of the representatives they may choose, to grant from time to time such supplies for the defence of the country as shall be judged necessary, so far as their abilities will allow.

" That the people in the colonies, who are to feel the immediate mischiefs of invasion and conquest by an enemy, in the loss of their estates, lives, and liberties, are likely to be better judges of the quantity of forces necessary to be raised and maintained, forts to be built and supported, and of their own abilities to bear the expence, than the parliament of England at so great a distance.

" That governors often come to the colonies merely to make fortunes, with which they intend to return to Britain; are not always men of the best abilities or integrity, have many of them no estate here, nor any natural connections with us, that should make them heartily concerned for our welfare; and might possibly be fond of raising and keeping up more forces than necessary, from the profits accruing to themselves, and to make provision for their friends and dependants.

" That the counsellors in most of the colonies being appointed by the crown, on the recommendation of governors, are often of small estates, frequently dependent on the governors for offices, and therefore too much under influence.

" That there is, therefore, great reason to be jealous of a power in such governors and councils, to raise such sums as they shall judge necessary,

necessary, by draft on the Lords of the Treasury, to be afterwards laid on the colonies by act of parliament, and paid by the people here; since they might abuse it by projecting useless expeditions, harassing the people, and taking them from their labour to execute such projects, merely to create offices and employments, and gratify their dependants, and divide profits.

" That the parliament of England is at a great distance, subject to be misinformed and misled by such governors and councils, whose united interests might probably secure them against the effect of any complaint from hence.

" That is supposed an undoubted right of Englishmen not to be taxed but by their own consent given through their representatives.

" That the colonies have no representatives in parliament.

" That to propose taxing them by parliament, and refuse them the liberty of choosing

a repre-

a representative council, to meet in the colonies, and consider and judge of the necessity of any general tax, and the quantum, shews a suspicion of their loyalty to the crown, or of their regard for their country, or of their common sense and understanding, which they have not deserved.

" That compelling the colonies to pay money without their consent, would be rather like raising contributions in an enemy's country, than taxing of Englishmen for their own public benefit.

" That it would be treating them as a conquered people, and not as true British subjects.

" That a tax laid by the representatives of the colonies might easily be lessened as the occasions should lessen, but being once laid by parliament under the influence of the representations made by governors, would probably be kept up and continued for the benefit of governors, to the grievous burden and discouragement of the colonies, and prevention of their growth and increase.

" That

" That a power in governors to march the inhabitants from one end of the British and French colonies to the other, being a country of at least 1500 miles square, without the approbation or consent of their representatives first obtained to such expeditions, might be grievous and ruinous to the people, and would put them on a footing with the subjects of France in Canada, that now groan under such oppression from their governor, who for two years past has harassed them with long and destructive marches to the Ohio.

" That if the colonies in a body may be well governed by governors and councils appointed by the crown, without representatives, particular colonies may as well or better be so governed; a tax may be laid on them all by act of parliament for support of government, and their assemblies may be dismissed as an useless part of the constitution.

" That the powers proposed by the Albany plan of union, to be vested in a Grand Council representative of the people, even with

with regard to military matters, are not so great as those the colonies of Rhode-Island and Connecticut are entrusted with by their charters, and have never abused; for by this plan, the president general is appointed by the crown, and controls all by his negative; but in those governments the people choose the governor, and yet allow him no negative.

"That the British colonies bordering on the French are properly frontiers of the British empire; and the frontiers of an empire are properly defended at the joint expence of the body of the people in such empire: it would now be thought hard by act of parliament to oblige the Cinque Ports or sea coasts of Britain to maintain the whole navy, because they are more immediately defended by it, not allowing them at the same time a vote in choosing members of the parliament; and if the frontiers in America must bear the expence of their own defence, it seems hard to allow them no share in voting the money, judging of the necessity and sum, or advising the measures.

"That

"That besides the taxes necessary for the defence of the frontiers, the colonies pay yearly great sums to the mother country unnoticed: for taxes paid in Britain by the landholder or artificer, must enter into and increase the price of the produce of land and of manufactures made of it; and great part of this is paid by consumers in the colonies, who thereby pay a considerable part of the British taxes.

" We are restrained in our trade with foreign nations; and where we could be supplied with any manufacture cheaper from them, but must buy the same dearer from Britain, the difference of price is a clear tax to Britain. We are obliged to carry great part of our produce directly to Britain, and where the duties there laid upon it lessen its price to the planter, or it sells for less than it would in foreign markets, the difference is a tax paid to Britain.

" Some manufactures we could make, but are forbidden, and must take them of British merchants; the whole price of these is a tax paid to Britain.

" By

"By our greatly increasing the demand and consumption of British manufactures, their price is considerably raised of late years; the advance is clear profit to Britain, and enables its people better to pay great taxes; and much of it being paid by us, is clear tax to Britain.

"In short, as we are not suffered to regulate our trade, and restrain the importation and consumption of British superfluities, (as Britain can the consumption of foreign superfluities,) our whole wealth centres finally among the merchants and inhabitants of Britain; and if we make them richer, and enable them better to pay their taxes, it is nearly the same as being taxed ourselves; and equally beneficial to the crown.

"These kind of secondary taxes, however, we do not complain of, though we have no share in the laying or disposing of them; but to pay immediate heavy taxes, in the laying, appropriation, and disposition of which we have no part, and which, perhaps, we may know to be as unnecessary as grievous, must seem hard measure to Englishmen, who cannot conceive, that by hazarding their lives and

and fortunes in subduing and settling new countries, extending the dominion and increasing the commerce of their mother nation; they have forfeited the native rights of Britons, which they think ought rather to be given them as due to such merit, if they had been before in a state of slavery.

" These, and such kind of things as these, I apprehend, will be thought and said by the people, if the proposed alteration of the Albany plan should take place. Then the administration of the Board of Governors and Council so appointed, not having any representative body of the people to approve and unite in its measures, and conciliate the minds of the people to them, will probably become suspected and odious; dangerous animosities and feuds will arise between the governors and governed, and every thing go into confusion.

" Perhaps I am too apprehensive in this matter; but having freely given my opinion and reasons, your Excellency can judge better than I whether there be any weight in them,

and

and the shortness of the time allowed me will, I hope, in some degree, excuse the imperfections of this scrawl.

"With the greatest respect and fidelity, I have the honour to be,
"Your Excellency's
"Most obedient, and most humble servant,
"B. Franklin."

"Sir, Boston, Dec. 22, 1754.
"Since the conversation your Excellency was pleased to honour me with, on the subject of uniting the colonies more intimately with Great Britain, by allowing them representatives in parliament, I have something further considered that matter, and am of opinion, that such an union would be very acceptable to the colonies, provided they had a reasonable number of representatives allowed them; and that all the old acts of parliament restraining the trade or cramping the manufactures of the colonies, be at the same time repealed, and the British subjects on this side the water put, in those respects, on the same footing with those in Great Britain, till the new parliament, representing the whole, shall think

think it for the interest of the whole to reenact some or all of them: it is not that I imagine so many representatives will be allowed the colonies, as to have any great weight by their numbers; but I think there might be sufficient to occasion those laws to be better and more impartially considered, and perhaps to overcome the private interest of a petty corporation, or of any particular set of artificers or traders in England, who heretofore seem, in some instances, to have been more regarded than all the colonies, or than was consistent with the general interest or best national good. I think too, that the government of the colonies by a parliament, in which they are fairly represented, would be vastly more agreeable to the people, than the method lately attempted to be introduced by royal instructions, as well as more agreeable to the nature of an English constitution, and to English liberty; and that such laws as now seem to bear hard on the colonies, would (when judged by such a parliament for the best interest of the whole) be more cheerfully submitted to, and more easily executed.

"I should hope too, that by such an union, the people of Great Britain, and the people of the colonies, would learn to consider themselves, not as belonging to different communities with different interests, but to one community with one interest, which I imagine would contribute to strengthen the whole, and greatly lessen the danger of future separations.

"It is, I suppose, agreed to be the general interest of any state, that its people be numerous and rich; men enough to fight in its defence, and enough to pay sufficient taxes to defray the charge; for these circumstances tend to the security of the state, and its protection from foreign power: but it seems not of so much importance whether the fighting be done by John or Thomas, or the tax paid by William or Charles. The iron manufacture employs and enriches British subjects; but is it of any importance to the state, whether the manufacturers live at Birmingham or Sheffield, or both, since they are still within its bounds, and their wealth and persons at its command? Could the Goodwin Sands

Sands be laid dry by banks, and land equal to a large country thereby gained to England, and prefently filled with Englifh inhabitants, would it be right to deprive fuch inhabitants of the common privileges enjoyed by other Englifhmen, the right of vending their produce in the fame ports, and of making their own fhoes, becaufe a merchant, or a fhoemaker, living on the old land, might fancy it more for his advantage to trade or make fhoes for them? Would this be right, even if the land were gained at the expence of the ftate? And would it not feem lefs right, if the charge and labour of gaining the additional territory to Britain had been borne by the fettlers themfelves? And would not the hardfhip appear yet greater, if the people of the new country fhould be allowed no reprefentatives in the parliament enacting fuch impofitions? Now I look on the colonies as fo many counties gained to Great Britain, and more advantageous to it than if they had been gained out of the fea around its coafts, and joined to its land: for being in different climates, they afford greater variety of produce,

duce, and materials for more manufactures; and being separated by the ocean, they increase much more its shipping and seamen; and since they are all included in the British empire, which has only extended itself by their means; and the strength and wealth of the parts is the strength and wealth of the whole; what imports it to the general state, whether a merchant, a smith, or a hatter, grow rich in *Old* or *New* England? And if, through increase of people, two smiths are wanted for one employed before, why may not the *new* smith be allowed to live and thrive in the *new country*, as well as the *old* one in the *old?* In fine, why should the countenance of a state be *partially* afforded to its people, unless it be most in favour of those who have most merit? And if there be any difference, those who have most contributed to enlarge Britain's empire and commerce, increase her strength, her wealth, and the numbers of her people, at the risk of their own lives and private fortunes, in new and strange countries, methinks ought rather to expect some preference.

" With

" With the greatest respect and esteem, I have the honour to be
" Your Excellency's
" Most obedient, and most humble servant,
" B. Franklin."

The north-western frontier being soon afterwards invaded by the enemy, it became necessary to take measures for the protection of the inhabitants. Dr. Franklin was ordered by the governor to take charge of this affair. Authority to raise men, and to appoint officers, was given to him. He immediately levied a body of troops, and marched to the part where their presence was necessary to check the enemy. He remained there some time, and did not leave his little army until required to attend the assembly of the province upon some important business.

The internal disputes between the proprietaries and the assembly still continuing, it was at length resolved, to present a petition to the King in council, upon the subject; and Dr. Franklin was appointed agent of the province, and to present it.

He departed from America in the month of June 1757. He presented the petition with which he was charged, and the matter was heard before the Privy Council. After an ample discussion, it was proposed to Dr. Franklin to engage, for the assembly, that the assessment of taxes should be so made, as that the proprietary estates should pay no more than a due proportion. To this he agreed, and tranquillity was at that time restored to the province.

During his residence in London, he was admitted a member of the Royal Society. And the Universities of Oxford, Edinburgh, and St. Andrews, conferred on him the degree of Doctor of Laws.

In the year 1760, upon the prospect of peace between Great Britain and France, the late Lord Bath wrote a tract, which he called " A Letter to two great Men." These were Mr. Pitt and the Duke of Newcastle. The subject of the letter was, the conditions of peace, which the writer thought should be insisted upon. He thought the possession of of Canada preferable to the acquisitions in the West Indies.

In answer to this pamphlet, there was another, called "Remarks upon it," written by Messieurs Burkes; in which the preference is given to Guadaloupe. (Martinico was not at that time taken.)

Dr. Franklin being of Lord Bath's opinion, wrote a reply to the "Remarks," which he intitled "The true Interest of Great Britain considered, with regard to her Colonies, and the Acquisitions of Canada and Guadaloupe;" in which he supported the arguments of Lord Bath.

In the year 1762, Dr. Franklin returned to America. He received the thanks of the Assembly of Pennsylvania, "as well for the faithful discharge of his duty to that province in particular, as for the many and important services done to America in general, during his residence in Great Britain." A compensation of five thousand pounds were voted to him for his services during the six years.

In the year 1764 he was again appointed agent to Great Britain.

The meafure, and the confequences of the American ftamp act, and the examination of Dr. Franklin before the Houfe of Commons, are all of them well known.

After the difputes on that fubject were fettled, he vifited feveral parts of Holland, Germany, and France.

In the year 1770, Dr. Franklin, together with the Hon. Thomas Walpole, banker in London, John Sargent, and Samuel Wharton, Efqrs. prefented a petition to the King and Council, for a grant of lands on the river Ohio in North America. The idea was to erect a new province in America. The defign had been mentioned to Lord Halifax fome years before, when his Lordfhip was at the head of the Board of Trade; and Lord Halifax approved of it very highly. The petitioners made many perfons of property fign; feveral of whom engaged to become proprietors, if the grant was obtained.

After

After the petition had lain some time before the Privy Council, it was, in the usual way, referred to the Board of Trade, to consider, and report upon it.

The following is a copy of the Report, which the Board of Trade made to the Lords of the Privy Council.

" Report of the Lords Commissioners for Trade and Plantations; on the Petition of the Honourable Thomas Walpole and his Associates, for a Grant of Lands on the River Ohio in North America.

" MY LORDS,

" Pursuant to your Lordships' order of the 25th May 1770, we have taken into our consideration the humble memorial of the Hon. Thomas Walpole, Benjamin Franklin, John Sargent, and Samuel Wharton, Esqrs. in behalf of themselves and their associates, setting forth, (among other things,) ' That
' they presented a petition to his Majesty in
' council, for a grant of lands in America
' *(parcel* of the lands purchased by govern-
' ment

' ment of the Indians) in confideration of a
' price to be paid in purchafe of the fame;
' *that in purfuance of a fuggeftion which arofe*
' *when the faid petition was under confideration*
' *of the Lords Commiffioners for Trade and*
' *Plantations*, the memorialifts prefented a
' petition to the Lords Commiffioners of
' the Treafury, propofing to purchafe a
' larger tract of land on the river Ohio in
' America, fufficient for a feparate govern-
' ment; whereupon their Lordfhips were
' pleafed to acquaint the memorialifts, they
' had no objection to accepting the propofals
' made by them with refpect to the pur-
' chafe-money and quit-rent to be paid for
' the faid tract of land, if it fhould be
' thought advifable by thofe departments
' of government, to whom it belonged to
' judge of the propriety of the grant, both in
' point of policy and juftice, that the grant
' fhould be made; in confequence whereof,
' the memorialifts humbly renew their ap-
' plication, that a grant of faid lands may
' be made to them, *referving therein to all*
' *perfons their juft and legal rights to any*
' *parts or parcels of faid lands which may be*
' *comprehended*

'*comprehended within the tract prayed for
' by the memorialists;*' whereupon we beg
leave to *report* to your Lordships,.

" I. That according to the description of
the tract of land prayed for by the memorialists, which description is annexed to their
memorial, it appears to us to contain part
of the dominion of Virginia, to the south
of the river Ohio, and to extend several
degrees of longitude westward from the
western ridge of the Appalachian mountains,
as will more fully appear to your Lordships
from the annexed sketch of the said tract,
which we have since caused to be deline-
ated with as much exactness as possible, and
herewith submit to your Lordships, to the
end that your Lordships may judge with the
greater precision of the situation of the lands
prayed for in the memorial.

" II. From this sketch your Lordships
will observe, that a very considerable part
of the lands prayed for lies beyond the line,
which has, in consequence of his Majesty's
orders for that purpose, been settled by treaty,

as

as well with the tribes of the Six Nations, and their confederates, as with the Cherokee Indians, as the boundary line between his Majesty's territories and their hunting-grounds: and as the faith of the crown is pledged in the most solemn manner both to the Six Nations and to the Cherokees, that notwithstanding the former of these nations had ceded the property in the lands to his Majesty, yet no settlements shall be made beyond that line, it is our duty to report to your Lordships our opinion, that it would on that account be highly improper to comply with the request of the memorial, *so far as it includes any lands beyond the said line.*

" It remains, therefore, that we report to your Lordships our opinion, how far it may consist with good policy and with justice, that his Majesty should comply with that part of the memorial which relates to those lands which are situated to the east of that line, and are part of the dominion of Virginia.

" III. And first with regard to the policy, we take leave to remind your Lordships of that

that principle which was adopted by this Board, and approved and confirmed by his Majesty, immediately after the treaty of Paris, *viz.* the confining the western extent of settlements to such a distance from the sea coast, as that those settlements should lie *within the reach of the trade and commerce of this kingdom*, upon which the strength and riches of it depend; and also of the exercise of that authority and jurisdiction, which was conceived to be necessary for the preservation of the colonies, in a due subordination to, and dependence upon, the mother country; and these we apprehend to have been two capital objects of his Majesty's proclamation of the 7th of October 1763, by which his Majesty declares it to be his royal will and pleasure to reserve under his sovereignty, protection, and dominion, for the *use* of the Indians, all the lands not included within the three new governments, the limits of which are described therein, as also all the lands and territories lying to the westward of the sources of the rivers which shall fall into the sea from the west and north-west, and by which all persons are forbid to make any purchases or settlements

tlements whatever, or to take poffeffion of any of the lands above referved, without fpecial licence for that purpofe.

" IV. It is true indeed, that partly from *want of precifion* in defcribing the line intended to be marked out by the proclamation of 1763, and partly from a confideration of juftice *in regard to legal titles to lands*, which had been fettled beyond that line, it has been fince thought fit to enter into engagements with the Indians, for fixing a more precife and determinate *boundary* between his Majefty's territories and their hunting-grounds.

" V. By this *boundary*, fo far as it regards the cafe now in queftion, your Lordfhips will obferve, that the hunting-grounds of the Indians are reduced within narrower limits than were fpecified by the proclamation of 1763; we beg leave however, to fubmit to your Lordfhips, that the fame principles of policy, in reference to fettlements *at fo great a diftance* from the fea-coaft *as to be out of the reach of all advantageous intercourfe with this kingdom*, continue to exift in their full force and

and spirit; and, though various propositions for erecting new colonies in the interior parts of America have been, in consequence of this extension of the boundary line, submitted to the consideration of government, (particularly in that part of the country wherein are situated the lands now prayed for, with a view to that object,) yet the dangers and disadvantages of complying with such proposals have been so obvious, as to defeat every attempt made for carrying them into execution.

" VI. Many objections, besides those which we have already stated, occur to us to propositions of this kind; but as *every argument* on this subject is *collected together with great force and precision*, in a representation made to his Majesty by the Commissioners for Trade and Plantations in March 1768, we beg leave to state them to your Lordships in their words.

" In that representation they deliver their opinion upon a proposition for settling new colonies in the interior country as follows, *viz.*

' The

' The propofition of forming inland colo-
' nies in America is, we humbly conceive,
' entirely new: it adopts principles in refpect
' to American fettlements, different from
' what have hitherto been the policy of this
' kingdom, and leads to a fyftem which, if
' purfued through all its confequences, is, in
' the prefent ftate of that country, of the
' greateft importance.

' The great object of colonizing upon the
' continent of North America, has been to
' improve and extend the commerce, naviga-
' tion, and manufactures of this kingdom,
' upon which its ftrength and fecurity de-
' pend.

' 1. By promoting the advantageous fifhery
' carried on upon the northern coaft.

' 2. By encouraging the growth and cul-
' ture of naval ftores, and of raw materials,
' to be tranfported hither in exchange for
' perfect manufactures and other merchan-
' dife.

' 3. By

' 3. By securing a supply of lumber, pro-
' visions, and other necessaries, for the sup-
' port of our establishments in the American
' islands.

' In order to answer these salutary purposes,
' it has been the policy of this kingdom to
' confine her settlements as much as possible
' to the sea-coast, and not to extend them to
' places inaccessible to shipping, and conse-
' quently more out of the reach of commerce;
' a plan which, at the same time that it se-
' cured the attainment of these commercial
' objects, had the further political advantage
' of guarding against all interfering of foreign
' powers, and of enabling this kingdom to
' keep up a superior naval force in those seas,
' by the actual possession of such rivers and
' harbours as were proper stations for fleets
' in time of war.

' Such, may it please your Majesty, have
' been the considerations inducing that plan
' of policy hitherto pursued in the settlement
' of your Majesty's American colonies, with
' which the private interest and sagacity of

' the

' the settlers co-operated from the first estab-
' lishments formed upon that continent. It
' was upon these principles, and with these
' views, that government undertook the
' settling of Nova Scotia in 1749; and it
' was from a view of the advantages repre-
' sented to arise from it in these different
' articles, that it was so liberally supported
' by the aid of parliament.

' The same motives, though operating in
' a less degree, and applying to fewer objects,
' did, as we humbly conceive, induce the
' forming the colonies of Georgia, East
' Florida, and West Florida, to the South,
' and the making those provincial arrange-
' ments in the proclamation of 1763, by
' which the interior country was left to the
' possession of the Indians.

' Having thus briefly stated what has been
' the policy of this kingdom in respect to co-
' lonizing in America, it may be necessary to
' take a cursory view of what has been the
' effect of it in those colonies, where there
' has been sufficient time for that effect to

' discover

'discover itself; because, if it shall appear
' from the present state of these settlements,
' and the progress they have made, that they
' are likely to produce the advantages above
' stated, it will, we humbly apprehend, be a
' very strong argument against forming settle-
' ments in the interior country; more espe-
' cially, when every advantage, derived from
' an established government, would naturally
' tend to draw the stream of population;
' fertility of soil and temperature of climate
' offering superior incitements to settlers,
' who, exposed to few hardships, and strug-
' gling with few difficulties, could, with little
' labour, earn an abundance for their own
' wants, but without a possibility of supplying
' ours with any considerable quantities. Nor
' would these inducements be confined in
' their operation to foreign emigrants, deter-
' mining their choice where to settle, but
' would act most powerfully upon the inhabit-
' ants of the northern and southern latitudes
' of your Majesty's American dominions;
' who, ever suffering under the opposite ex-
' tremes of heat and cold, would be equally
' tempted by a moderate climate to abandon

' latitudes peculiarly adapted to the produc-
' tion of those things, which are by Nature
' denied to us; and for the whole of which
' we should, without their assistance, stand
' indebted to, and dependent upon other
' countries.

' It is well known that antecedent to the
' year 1749, all that part of the sea-coast of
' the British empire in America, which ex-
' tends north-east from the province of Main
' to Canceau in Nova Scotia, and from thence
' to the mouth of St. Laurence river, lay
' waste and neglected; though naturally af-
' fording, or capable by art of producing,
' every species of naval stores; the seas
' abounding with whale, cod, and other va-
' luable fish, and having many great rivers,
' bays, and harbours, fit for the reception of
' ships of war. Thus circumstanced, a con-
' sideration of the great commercial advan-
' tages which would follow from securing the
' possession of this country, combined with
' the evidence of the value set upon it by our
' enemies, who, during the war which ter-
' minated at that period, had, at an immense
' expence,

' expence, attempted to wreſt it from us, in-
' duced that plan, for the ſettlement of Nova
' Scotia, to which we have before referred;
' and which, being proſecuted with vigour,
' though at a very large expence to this king-
' dom, ſecured the poſſeſſion of that pro-
' vince, and formed thoſe eſtabliſhments
' which contributed ſo greatly to facilitate
' and promote the ſucceſs of your Majeſty's
' arms in the late war.

' The eſtabliſhment of government in this
' part of America, having opened to the view
' and information of your Majeſty's ſubjects
' in other colonies the great commercial ad-
' vantages to be derived from it, induced a
' zeal for migration; and aſſociations were
' formed for taking up lands, and making
' ſettlements, in this province, by principal
' perſons reſiding in theſe colonies.

' In conſequence of theſe aſſociations, up-
' wards of ten thouſand ſouls have paſſed
' from thoſe colonies into Nova Scotia; who
' have either engaged in the fiſheries, or be-
' come exporters of lumber and proviſions to

' the West Indies. And further settlements,
' to the extent of twenty-one townships, of
' one hundred thousand acres each, have
' been engaged to be made there, by many of
' the principal persons in Pennsylvania, whose
' names and association for that purpose now
' lie before your Majesty in council.

' The government of Massachusetts Bay,
' as well as the proprietors of large tracts to
' the eastward of the province of Main, ex-
' cited by the success of these settlements, are
' giving every encouragement to the like
' settlements in that valuable country, lying
' between them and Nova Scotia; and the
' proprietors of the twelve townships lately
' laid out there, by the Massachusetts govern-
' ment, now solicit your Majesty for a con-
' firmation of their title.

' Such, may it please your Majesty, is the
' present state of the progress making in the
' settlement of the northern parts of the sea-
' coasts of North America, in consequence of
' what appears to have been the policy
' adopted by this kingdom. And many per-
' sons

' sons of rank and substance here are pro-
' ceeding to carry into execution the plan
' which your Majesty (pursuing the same
' principles of commercial policy) has ap-
' proved for the settlement of the islands of
' St. John and Cape Breton, and of the new
' established colonies to the south. And,
' therefore, as we are fully convinced, that
' the encouraging settlements upon the sea-
' coast of North America is founded in the
' true principles of commercial policy; as we
' find upon examination, that the happy ef-
' fects of that policy are now beginning to
' open themselves, in the establishment of
' these branches of commerce, culture, and
' navigation, upon which the strength,
' wealth, and security of this kingdom de-
' pend; we cannot be of opinion that it
' would in any view be advisable to divest
' your Majesty's subjects in America from
' the pursuit of those important objects, by
' adopting measures of a new policy, *at an
' expence to this kingdom, which in its present
' state it is unable to bear.*

P 4 ' This,

' This, may it please your Majesty, being
' the light in which we view the propofition
' of colonizing in the interior country, con-
' fidered as a general principle of policy; we
' fhall, in the next place, proceed to examine
' the feveral arguments urged in fupport of
' the particular eftablifhments now recom-
' mended.

' Thefe arguments appear to us reducible
' to the following general propofitions, viz.

' Firft, That fuch colonies will promote
' population, and increafe the demands for,
' and confumption of Britifh manufactures.

' Secondly, That they will fecure the fur
' trade, and prevent an illicit trade, or inter-
' fering of French or Spaniards with the
' Indians.

' Thirdly, That they will be a defence
' and protection to the old colonies againft
' the Indians.

' Fourthly,

'Fourthly, That they will contribute to
' lessen the present heavy expence of supply-
' ing provisions to the different forts and gar-
' risons.

' Lastly, That they are necessary in respect
' to the inhabitants already residing in those
' places where they are proposed to be esta-
' blished, who require some form of civil go-
' vernment.

' After what we have already stated with
' respect to the policy of encouraging colo-
' nies in the interior country as a general
' principle, we trust it will not be necessary
' to enter into an ample discussion of the ar-
' guments brought to support the foregoing
' propositions.

' We admit as an undeniable principle of
' true policy, that with a view to prevent
' manufactures, it is necessary and proper to
' open an extent of territory for colonization
' proportioned to the increase of people, as a
' large number of inhabitants, cooped up in
' narrow limits, without a sufficiency of land
' for

'for produce, would be compelled to convert
'their attention and induſtry to manufac-
'tures: but we ſubmit whether the encou-
'ragement given to the ſettlement of the colo-
'nies upon the ſea-coaſt, and the effect which
'ſuch encouragement has had, have not' al-
'ready effectually provided for this object, as
'well as for increaſing the demand for, and
'conſumption of Britiſh manufactures, an
'advantage which, in our humble opinion,
'would not be promoted by theſe new colo-
'nies, which being propoſed to be eſtabliſhed,
'at the diſtance of *above fifteen hundred miles
'from the ſea*, and in places which, upon the
'fulleſt evidence, are found to be utterly in-
'acceſſible to ſhipping, will, from their in-
'ability to find returns wherewith to pay for
'the manufactures of Great Britain, be pro-
'bably led to manufacture for themſelves; a
'conſequence which experience ſhews has
'conſtantly attended in greater or leſſer de-
'gree every inland ſettlement; and therefore
'ought, in our humble opinion, to be care-
'fully guarded againſt, by *encouraging* the
'ſettlement of that extenſive tract of ſea-coaſt
'hitherto unoccupied; *which, together with*

'the

' *the liberty that the inhabitants of the middle*
' *colonies will have* (in confequence *of the*
' *propofed boundary line with the Indians*) of
' *gradually extending themfelves backwards*,
' will more effectually and beneficially anfwer
' the object of encouraging population and
' confumption, than the erection of new go-
' vernments; fuch gradual extenfion might
' through the medium of a continued popu-
' lation, upon even the fame extent of terri-
' tory, preferve a communication of mutual
' commercial benefits between its extremeft
' parts and Great Britain, *impoffible* to *exift in*
' *colonies feparated by immenfe tracts of unpeo-*
' *pled defart*.—As to the effect which it is
' fuppofed the colonies may have to increafe
' and promote the fur trade, and to prevent
' all contraband trade or intercourfe between
' the Indians under your Majefty's protection,
' and the French or Spaniards; it does appear
' to us, that the extenfion of the fur trade
' depends entirely upon the Indians being
' undifturbed in the poffeffion of their hunt-
' ing-grounds; that all colonizing does in its
' nature, and muft in its confequences, ope-
' rate

' rate to the prejudice of that branch of
' commerce, and that the French and Spaniard
' would be left in poffeffion of a great part of
' what remained; as New Orleans would ftill
' continue the heft and fureft market.

' As to the protection which it is fuppofed
' thefe new colonies may be capable of af-
' fording to the old ones, it will, in our opi-
' nion, appear on the flighteft view of their
' fituation, that fo far from affording protec-
' tion to the old colonies, they will ftand
' moft in need of it themfelves.

' It cannot be denied, that new colonies
' would be of advantage in raifing provifions
' for the fupply of fuch forts and garrifons
' as may be kept up in the neighbourhood of
' them; but as the degree of utility will be
' proportioned to the number and fituation of
' thefe forts and garrifons, which upon the
' refult of the prefent inquiry it may be
' thought advifable to continue, fo the force
' of the argument will depend upon that
' event.

' The

' The present French inhabitants in the
' neighbourhood of the Lakes, will, in our
' humble opinion, be sufficient to furnish
' with provisions whatever posts may be ne-
' cessary to be continued there; and as there
' are also French inhabitants settled in some
' parts of the country lying upon the Mis-
' sissippi, between the rivers Illinois and the
' Ohio, it is to be hoped that a sufficient
' number of these may be induced to fix
' their abode, where the same convenience
' and advantage may be derived from them;
' but if no such circumstance were to exist,
' and no such assistance to be expected
' from it, the objections stated to the plan
' now under our consideration are superior to
' this, or any other advantage it can produce;
' and although civil establishments have fre-
' quently rendered the expence of an armed
' force necessary for their protection, one
' of the many objections to these now pro-
' posed, yet we humbly presume there never
' has been an instance of a government in-
' stituted merely with a view to supply a
' body of troops with suitable provisions;
' nor is it necessary in these instances for the
' settle-

'settlements, already existing, as above de-
'scribed, which being formed under mili-
'tary establishments, and ever subjected to
'military authority, do not, in our humble
'opinion, require any other superintendence
'than that of the military officers command-
'ing at these posts.'

" In addition to this opinion of the Board of Trade, expressed in the foregoing recital, we further beg leave to refer your Lordships to the opinion of the Commander in Chief of his Majesty's forces in North America, who, in a letter laid before us by the Earl of Hillsborough, delivers his sentiments with regard to the settlements in the interior parts of America in the following words, *viz.*

" VII. 'As to increasing the settlements to
'respectable provinces, and to colonization
'*in general terms* in the *remote* countries, I
'conceive it altogether inconsistent with
'sound policy; for there is little appearance
'that the advantages will arise from it which
'nations expect when they send out colonies
  'into

' into *foreign countries*; they can give no en-
' couragement to the fishery, and though the
' country might afford some kind of naval
' stores, the distance would be too far to
' transport them; and for the same reason
' they could not supply the sugar islands
' with lumber and provisions. As for the
' raising wine, silk, and other commodities,
' the same may be said of the present colonies
' without planting others for the purpose at
' so vast a distance; but on the supposition
' that they would be raised, their very long
' transportation must probably make them
' too dear for any market. I do not appre-
' hend the inhabitants could have any com-
' modities to barter for manufactures except
' skins and furs, which will naturally decrease
' as the country increases in people, and the
' deserts are cultivated; so that in the course
' of a few years necessity would force them
' to provide manufactures of some kind for
' themselves; and when all connection up-
' held by commerce with the mother country
' shall cease, it may be expected, that an in-
' dependency on her government will soon
' follow; the pretence of forming barriers

' will have no end; wherever we settle, how-
' ever remote, there must be a frontier; and
' there is room enough for the colonists to
' spread within our present limits, for a cen-
' tury to come. If we reflect how the peo-
' ple of themselves have gradually retired
' from the coast, we shall be convinced they
' want no encouragement to desert sea-coasts,
' and go into the back countries, where the
' lands are better, and got upon easier terms;
' they are already almost out of the reach of
' law and government; neither the endea-
' vours of government, or fear of Indians,
' has kept them properly within bounds;
' and it is apparently most for the interest of
' Great Britain to confine the colonies on
' the side of the back country, and to direct
' their settlements along the sea-coast, where
' millions of acres are yet uncultivated. The
' lower provinces are still thinly inhabited,
' and not brought to the point of perfection
' that has been aimed at for the mutual be-
' nefit of Great Britain and themselves. Al-
' though America may supply the mother
' country with many articles, few of them
' are yet supplied in quantities equal to her

' con-

'consumption; the quantity of iron transported is not great, of hemp very small, and there are many other commodities not necessary to enumerate, which America has not yet been able to raise, notwithstanding the encouragement given her by bounties and premiums. The laying open new tracts of fertile territory in moderate climates might lessen her present produce; for it is the passion of every man to be a landholder, and the people have a natural disposition to rove in search of good lands, however distant. It may be a question likewise, whether colonization of the kind could be effected *without an Indian war, and fighting for every inch of ground*. The Indians have long been jealous of our power, and have no patience in seeing us approach their towns, and settle upon their hunting-grounds; atonements may be made for a fraud discovered in a trader, and even the murder of some of their tribes, but *encroachments* upon their lands have often produced serious consequences. The springs of the last general war are to be discovered near the Allegany mountains, and upon the banks of the Ohio.

' It is so obvious, that settlers might raise
' provisions to feed the troops cheaper than it
' can be transported from the country below,
' that it is not necessary to explain it; but
' I must own I know no other use in settle-
' ments, or can give any other reason for
' supporting forts, than to protect the set-
' tlements, and keep the settlers in subjection
' to government.

' I conceive, that to procure all the com-
' merce it will afford, and as little expence
' to ourselves as we can, is the only object
' we shall have in view in the interior coun-
' try for a century to come; and I imagine
' it might be effected, by proper manage-
' ment, without either forts or settlements.
' Our manufactures are as much desired by
' the Indians, as their peltry is sought for by
' us; what was originally deemed a super-
' fluity, or a luxury by the natives, is now
' become a necessary; they are disused to
' the bow, and can neither hunt, or make
' war without fire-arms, powder, and lead.
' The British provinces can only supply
' them with their necessaries, which they
' know, and for their own sakes would pro-
' tect

' test the trader, which they actually do at
' present. It would remain with us to pre-
' vent the trader's being guilty of frauds and
' impositions, and to pursue the same me-
' thods to that end, as are taken in the
' southern district; and I must confess,
' though the plan pursued in that district
' might be improved by proper laws to sup-
' port it, that I do not know a better or more
' œconomical plan for the management of
' trade; there are neither forts nor settle-
' ments in the southern department, and
' there are both in the northern department;
' and your Lordships will be the best judge,
' which of them has given you the least
' trouble; in which we have had the fewest
' quarrels with, or complaints from the In-
' dians.

' I know of nothing so liable to bring on
' a serious quarrel with Indians *as an invasion*
' *of their property.* Let the savages enjoy
' their deserts in quiet; little bickerings that
' may unavoidably sometimes happen, may
' soon be accommodated; and I am of opi-
' nion, independent of the motives of com-
' mon justice and humanity, that the prin-
' ciples

'ciples of interest and policy should induce
'us rather to protect than molest them:
'were they driven from their forests, the
'peltry trade would decrease; and it is *not
impossible* that worse savages would take
'refuge in them, for they might then become
'the asylum of fugitive negroes, and idle
'vagabonds, escaped from justice, who in
'time might become formidable, and subsist
'by rapine, and plundering the lower coun-
'tries.'

"VIII. The opinions delivered in the foregoing recitals are so accurate and precise, as to make it almost unnecessary to add any thing more: but we beg leave to lay before your Lordships the sentiments of his Majesty's Governor of Georgia, upon the subject of large grants in the interior parts of America, whose knowledge and experience in the affairs of the colonies give great weight to his opinion.

"In a letter to us, on the subject of th mischiefs attending such grants, he expresse himself in the following manner, viz.

'An

‘ And now, my Lords, I beg your patience
‘ a moment, while I confider this matter in
‘ a more extenfive point of view, and go a
‘ little further in declaring my fentiments
‘ and opinion, with refpect to the granting
‘ of large bodies of land, in the back parts
‘ of the province of Georgia, or in any other
‘ of his Majefty's northern colonies, at a dif-
‘ tance from the fea-coaft, or from fuch parts
‘ of any province as are already fettled and
‘ inhabited.

‘ And this matter, my Lords, appears to
‘ me, in a very ferious and alarming light;
‘ and I humbly conceive may be attended
‘ with the greateft and worft of confequences;
‘ for, my Lords, if a vaft territory be granted
‘ to any fet of gentlemen, who really mean
‘ to people it, and actually do fo, it muft
‘ draw and carry out a great number of peo-
‘ ple from Great Britain; and I apprehend
‘ they will foon become a kind of feparate and
‘ independent people, and who will fet up
‘ for themfelves; that they will foon have
‘ manufactures of their own; that they will
‘ neither take fupplies from the mother coun-

' try, or from the provinces, at the back of
' which they are settled; that being at a dis-
' tance from the seat of government, courts,
' magistrates, &c. &c. they will be out of
' the reach and control of law and govern-
' ment; that it will become a receptacle
' and kind of asylum for offenders, who will
' fly from justice to such new country or
' colony; and therefore crimes and offences
' will be committed, not only by the inhabit-
' ants of such new settlements, but elsewhere,
' and pass with impunity; and that in pro-
' cess of time (and perhaps at no great dis-
' tance) they will become formidable enough
' to oppose his Majesty's authority, disturb
' government, and even give law to the
' other or first settled part of the country,
' and throw every thing into confusion.

' My Lords, I hope I shall not be thought
' impertinent, when I give my opinion freely,
' in a matter of so great consequence, as I
' conceive this to be; and, my Lords, I ap-
' prehend, that in all the American colonies,
' great care should be taken, that the lands on
' the sea-coast should be thick settled with
' inhabit-

inhabitants, and well cultivated and im-
' proved; and that the settlements should be
' gradually extended back into the province,
' and as much connected as possible, to keep
' the people together in as narrow a compass
' *as the nature of the lands and state of things*
' *will admit of;* and by which means there
' would probably become only one general
' view and interest amongst them, and the
' power of government and law would of
' course naturally and easily go with them,
' and matters thereby properly regulated, and
' kept in due order and obedience; and they
' would have no idea of resisting or trans-
' gressing either without being amenable to
' justice, and subject to punishment for any
' offences they may commit.

' But, my Lords, to suffer a kind of *pro-*
' *vince within a province*, and one that may,
' indeed must in process of time become su-
' perior, and too big for the head or original
' settlement or seat of government, to me con-
' veys with it many ideas of consequence, of
' such a nature, as I apprehend are extremely
' dangerous and improper, and it would be

' the

' the policy of government to avoid and pre-
' vent, whilft in their power to do fo.

' My ideas, my Lords, are not chimerical;
' I know fomething of the fituation and ftate
' of things in America; and from fome little
' occurrences or inftances that have already
' really happened, I can very eafily figure to
' myfelf what may, and, in fhort, what
' will certainly happen, if not prevented in
' time.'

"IX. At the fame time that we fubmit the foregoing reafoning againft colonization in the interior country to your Lordfhips' confideration, it is proper we fhould take notice of one argument, which has been invariably held forth in fupport of every propofition of this nature, and upon which the prefent proponents appear to lay great ftrefs. It is urged, that fuch is the ftate of the country now propofed to be granted, and erected into a feparate government, that no endeavours on the part of the crown can avail, to prevent its being fettled by thofe who, by the increafe of population in the middle colonies, are continually

nually emigrating to the westward, and forming themselves into colonies in that country, without the intervention or control of government, and who, if suffered to continue in that lawless state of anarchy and confusion, will commit such abuses as cannot fail of involving us in quarrel and dispute with the Indians, and thereby endangering the security of his Majesty's colonies.

" We admit, that this is an argument that deserves attention; and we rather take notice of it in this place, because some of the objections stated by Governor Wright *lose their force, upon the supposition that the grants against which he argues are to be erected into separate governments.* But we are clearly of opinion, that his arguments do, in the general view of them, as applied to the question of granting lands in the interior parts of America, stand unanswerable; and *admitting* that the settlers in the country in question are *as numerous as report states them to be,* yet we submit to your Lordships, that this is a fact which does, in the nature of it, operate strongly in point of argument *against*
what

what is proposed; for if the foregoing reasoning has any weight, it certainly ought to induce your Lordships to advise his Majesty to take every method to *check* the progress of these settlements, and *not* to make such grants of the land as will have an immediate tendency to encourage them; a measure which we conceive is altogether as unnecessary as it is impolitic, as we see nothing to hinder the government of Virginia from extending the laws and constitution of that colony to such persons as may have already settled there *under legal titles*.

" X. And there is one objection suggested by Governor Wright to the extension of settlements in the interior country, which, we submit, deserves your Lordships' particular attention, viz. the encouragement that is thereby held out to the emigration of his Majesty's European subjects; an argument which, in the present peculiar situation of this kingdom, demands very serious consideration, and has for some time past had so great weight with this Board, that it has induced us to deny our concurrence to many proposals

proposals for grants of land, even in those parts of the continent of America where, in all other respects, we are of opinion that it consists with the true policy of this kingdom to encourage settlements; and this consideration of the certain bad consequences which must result from a continuance of such emigrations, as have lately taken place from various parts of his Majesty's European dominions, added to the constant drains to Africa, to the East Indies, and to the new ceded islands, will, we trust, with what has been before stated, be a sufficient answer to every argument that can be urged in support of the present memorial, so far as regards the consideration of it in point of policy.

" XI. With regard to the propriety in point of *justice* of making the grant desired, we presume this consideration can have reference only to the case of such persons who have already possession of lands in that part of the country under legal titles derived from grants made by the Governor and Council of Virginia; upon which case we have only to observe, that it does appear to us, that there

are

are *some* such possessions held by persons who are not parties to the present memorial; and therefore, if your Lordships shall be of opinion, that the making the grant desired would, notwithstanding the reservation proposed in respect to such titles, have the effect to disturb those possessions, or to expose the proprietors to suit and litigation, we do conceive, that, in that case, the grant would be objectionable in point of justice.

" XII. Upon the whole, therefore, we cannot recommend to your Lordships to advise his Majesty to comply with the prayer of this memorial, either as to the erection of any parts of the lands into a separate government, or the making a grant of them to the memorialists; but, on the contrary, we are of opinion, that settlements in that distant part of the country should be as much discouraged as possible; and that, in order thereto, it will be expedient, not only that the orders which have been given to the Governor of Virginia, not to make any further grants beyond the line prescribed by the proclamation of 1763, should be continued and enforced, but that
another

another proclamation should be issued, declaratory of his Majesty's resolution not to allow, for the *present*, any new settlements beyond that line, and to forbid all persons from taking up or settling any lands in that part of the country.

" We are, my Lords,
 " Your Lordships' most obedient
  " and most humble servants.
" Whitehall, April 15, 1772."

To the preceding Report of the Board of Trade, Dr. Franklin wrote an elaborate answer, in the composition of which, he took great pains and bestowed much time and attention. If there were no other reasons, these would be sufficient to recommend it to the reader's notice. But there are others of a more weighty and important nature. The arguments and facts contained in it were found to be so strong, and the deductions from them so forcible, that when the petition and the report were taken into consideration in the Privy Council, which was on the first day of July 1772, their Lordships decided in favour of the petition. It was not often that the

Privy

Privy Council decided againſt reports from the Board of Trade.

Lord Hillſborough, who was at this time at the head of the Board of Trade, and conſequently had a principal ſhare in drawing up the report, was ſo much offended by the deciſion of the Privy Council, that he reſigned upon it. He reſigned for that reaſon only. He had conceived an idea, and was forming the plan of a boundary line to be drawn from the Hudſon's river to the Miſſiſſippi, and thereby confining the Britiſh colonies between that line and the ocean, ſimilar to the ſcheme of the French after the peace of Aix-la-Chapelle, which brought on the war of 1756. His favourite project being thus defeated, he quitted the miniſtry.

Dr. Franklin's anſwer to the Report of the Board of Trade was intended to have been publiſhed, but Lord Hillſborough reſigning, Dr. Franklin ſtopped the ſale on the morning of the publication, when not above *five* copies had been diſpoſed of: from one of which the following copy is taken.

To

To the above reasons it will not be improper to add, that it may be considered a valuable historical document of the origin of a new province that already bids fair to become one of the largest and most opulent on that great continent.

Observations on, and Answers to, the foregoing Report.

" I. The first paragraph of the Report, we apprehend, was intended to establish two propositions as facts; *viz.*

" First, That the tract of land agreed for with the Lords Commissioners of the Treasury, contains *part* of the dominion of Virginia.

" Second, That it extends several degrees of longitude *westward* from the western ridge of the *Allegany* mountains.

" On the first proposition we shall only remark, that no part of the above tract is to the *eastward* of the Allegany mountains;— and that these mountains must be considered as the true western boundary of *Virginia*;— for the King was *not* seised and possessed of a right *to the country westward* of the mountains, until his Majesty purchased it, in the year 1768, from the Six Nations: and since that time, there has not been any annexation of such purchase, or of any part thereof, to the colony of Virginia.

" On the second proposition,——we shall just observe, that the Lords Commissioners for Trade and Plantations appear to us to be as erroneous in this as in the former proposition; for their Lordships say, that the tract of land under consideration *extends several degrees* of longitude *westward*. The truth is, that it is not more, on a medium, than one degree and a half of longitude from the western ridge of the Allegany mountains to the river Ohio.

" II. It appears by the second paragraph, as if the Lords Commissioners for Trade and Plantations apprehended,——that the lands south-westerly of the *boundary line*, marked on a map annexed to their Lordships' *Report*,——
were

were either claimed by the Cherokees, or were their hunting-grounds, or were the hunting-grounds of the Six Nations and their confederates.

" As to any claim of the Cherokees to the above country, it is altogether new and indefensible; and never was heard of until the appointment of Mr. Stewart to the superintendency of the southern colonies, about the year 1764; and this, we flatter ourselves, will not only be obvious from the following state of facts, but that the right to *all the country* on the southerly side of the river Ohio, quite to the Cherokee river, is *now* undoubtedly vested in the King, by the grant which the Six Nations made to his Majesty at Fort Stanwix, in November 1768. In short, the lands from the *Great Kenhawa* to the *Cherokee river* never were either the dwelling or hunting-grounds of the *Cherokees*;—but formerly belonged to, and were inhabited by the *Shawaneffe*, until such time as they were conquered by the Six Nations.

" Mr.

"Mr. Colden, the present Lieutenant Governor of New York, in his History of the Five Nations, observes, that about the year 1664, 'the Five Nations being amply supplied 'by the English with fire-arms and ammu- 'nition, gave a full swing to their warlike 'genius. They carried their arms *as far* '*south as Carolina*, to the northward of New 'England, and *as far west as the river Mis-* '*sissippi*, over a vast country,—which ex- 'tended 1200 miles in length from north to 'south, and 600 miles in breadth,—where they 'entirely destroyed whole nations, of whom 'there are no accounts remaining among the 'English.'

"In 1701,—the Five Nations put all their hunting-lands under the protection of the English, as appears by the records, and by the recital and confirmation thereof, in their deed to the King of the 4th September 1726;—and Governor Pownal, who many years ago diligently searched into the rights of the natives, and in particular into those of the northern confederacy, says, in his book intitled, the *Administration of the Colonies*,
'The

' The right of the Five Nation confederacy
' to the hunting-*lands of Ohio*, Ticûckfou-
' chrondite and Scaniaderiada, by the con-
' queſt they made, in ſubduing the *Shaŏanaes*,
' Delawares, (as we call them,) Twictwees,
' and Oilinois, may be fairly proved, as
' they ſtood poſſeſſed thereof at the peace
' of Reſwick 1697.' And confirmatory
hereof, Mr. Lewis Evans, a gentleman of
great American knowledge, in his map of the
middle colonies, publiſhed in America in the
year 1755, has laid down the country on the
ſouth-eaſterly ſide of the river Ohio, *as the
hunting-lands of the Six Nations;* and in his
analyſis to this map, he expreſsly ſays,—
' The *Shawaneſſe*, who were formerly one of
' the moſt conſiderable nations of thoſe parts
' of America, whoſe ſeat extended from *Ken-*
' *tucke* ſouth-weſtward to the Miſſiſſippi, have
' been ſubdued by the confederates, (or Six
' Nations,) *and the country ſince became their
' property.* No nation,' Mr. Evans adds,
' held out with greater reſolution and bravery;
' and although they have been ſcattered in
' all parts for a while, they are again collected
' on *Ohio*, under the dominion of the confe-
' derates.'

"At a congress held in the year 1744, by the provinces of Pennsylvania, Maryland, and Virginia, with the Six Nations,—the Commissioners of Virginia, in a speech to the Sachems and Warriors of that confederacy, say, 'Tell us what nations of Indians you 'conquered any lands from in Virginia, how 'long it is since, and what possession you 'have had; and if it does appear, that there 'is any land on the *borders* of Virginia that 'the Six Nations have a right to, we are 'willing to make you satisfaction.'

"To this speech the Six Nations gave the following animated and decisive answer:— 'All the world knows we conquered the 'several nations living on Sasquehanna, Co- 'hongoranto [*i.e.* Powtomack] *and on the* '*back of the great mountains in Virginia;*— ''the Conoy-uck-suck-roona, Cock-now-was- 'roonan, Toboa-irough-roonan, and Connut- 'skin-ough-roonaw *feel* the effects of our con- 'quests; being now a part of our nations, 'and their lands at *our* disposal. We know 'very well, it hath often been said by the 'Virginians, that the King of England and 'the people of that colony conquered the

' people who lived there; but it is not true.
' We will allow, they conquered the Sach-
' dagughronaw, and drove back the Tufka-
' roras; [the firft refided near the branches
' of James's River in Virginia, and the latter
' on thefe branches;] and that they have, on
' that account, a right to fome parts of Vir-
' ginia; *but as to what lies beyond the moun-*
' *tains, we conquered the nations refiding there,*
' *and that land,* if the Virginians ever get a
' *good right to it, it muft be by us.*'

" In the year 1750, the French feized four Englifh traders, who were trading with the Six Nations, Shawaneffe and Delawares, on the waters of the Ohio, and fent them prifoners to Quebec, and from thence to France.

" In 1754, the French took a formal poffeffion of the river Ohio, and built forts at Venango,—at the confluence of the Ohio and Monongehela, and at the *mouth of the Cherokee river.*

" In 1755, General Braddock was fent to America with an army to remove the French from

from their possessions over the Allegany mountains, and on the river Ohio; and on his arrival at Alexandria, held a council of war with the Governors of Virginia, Maryland, Pennsylvania, New York, and the Massachusett's Bay;—and as these gentlemen well knew, that the country claimed by the French, *over the Allegany mountains, and south-westerly to the river Mississippi*, was the unquestionable property of the *Six Nations*, and *not* of the Cherokees, or any other tribe of Indians,—the General gave instructions to Sir William Johnson, to call together the Indians of the *Six Nations*, and lay before them their before-mentioned grant to the King in 1726,—wherein they had put all their hunting-lands *under his Majesty's protection; to be guaranteed to them, and to their use*:—And as General Braddock's instructions are clearly declaratory of the right of the Six Nations to the lands under consideration, we shall here transcribe the conclusive words of them:—
' And it appearing that the French have,
' from time to time, by fraud and violence,
' built strong forts *within the limits of the said*
' *lands*, contrary to the covenant chain of
' the

' the said deed and treaties, you are, in my
' name, to assure the said nations, that I am
' come by his Majesty's order, to destroy all
' the said forts, and to build such others
' *as shall protect and secure the said lands to*
' *them, their heirs and successors for ever,*
' according to the intent and spirit of the
' said treaty; and I do therefore call upon
' them to take up the hatchet, *and come and*
' *take possession of their own lands.*'

" That General Braddock and the American Governors were not singular in their opinion, as to the right of the Six Nations to the land *over* the Allegany mountains, and on both sides of the river Ohio, quite to the Mississippi, is evident, from the memorials which passed between the British and French courts in 1755.

" In a memorial delivered by the King's ministers on the 7th June 1755, to the Duke Mirepoix, relative to the pretensions of France to the above-mentioned lands, they very justly observed—' As to the exposition, which is
' made in the French memorial of the 15th
' article

'article of the treaty of Utrecht, the court
'of Great Britain does not think it can have
'any foundation, either by the words or the
'intention of this treaty.

'1st, The court of Great Britain can-
'not allow of this article, relating only to
'the persons of the savages, and *not to their
'country:* the words of this treaty are clear
'and precise; that is to say, the *Five Nations*,
'or Cantons, are subject to the dominion of
'Great Britain,—which, by the received ex-
'position of all treaties, must relate to the
'*country*, as well to the persons of the in-
'habitants;—it is what France has acknow-
'ledged in the most solemn manner:—she
'has well weighed the importance of this
'acknowledgment, at the time of signing
'this treaty, and Great Britain can never
'give it up. The countries possessed by
'these Indians *are very well known, and are
'not at all so undetermined,* as it is pretended
'in the memorial: they *possess* and *make them
'over, as other proprietors do, in all other
'places.*'

'5th,

' 5th, Whatever pretext might be al-
' ledged by France, in considering these coun-
' tries as the appurtenances of Canada; *it
' is a certain truth, that they have belonged,*
' *and* (as they have not been given up, *or*
' *made over* to the English) *belong still to the*
' *same Indian nations*; which, by the 15th
' article of the treaty of Utrecht, France
' agreed not to molest,—Nullo in posterum
' impedimento, aut molestia afficiant.'

' Notwithstanding all that has been ad-
' vanced in this article, the court of Great
' Britain *cannot* agree to France having the
' least title to the river Ohio, and the *terri-*
' *tory in question.*' [*N. B.* This was *all* the
country from the Allegany mountains to the
Ohio, and down the same, and on both sides
thereof to the river Mississippi.]

' Even that of possession is not, nor can
' it be alleged on this occasion; since France
' cannot pretend to have had any such before
' the treaty of Aix-la-Chapelle, nor since,
' unless it be that of certain *forts,* unjustly
' erected lately *on the lands which evidently*
' *belong*

'*belong to the Five Nations,* or which thefe
' have made over to the Crown of Great
' Britain or its fubjects, as may be proved by
' treaties and acts of the greateft authority.—
' *What* the court of Great Britain *maintained,*
' *and what it infifts upon,* is, That the Five
' Nations of the Iroquois, acknowledged by
' France, *are,* by origin, or *by right of conqueft*
' the *lawful proprietors of the river Ohio, and*
' *the territory in queftion:* and as to the ter-
' ritory which has been *yielded and made over*
' *by thefe people* to Great Britain, (which can-
' not but be owned muft be the moft juft
' and lawful manner of making an acquifition
' of this fort,) fhe reclaims it, as belonging to
' her, having continued cultivating it for
' above 20 years paft, and having made fet-
' tlements in feveral parts of it, from the
' fources even of the Ohio to Pichawillanes,
' in the centre of the territory between the
' Ohio and the Wabache.'

"In 1755, the Lords Commiffioners for Trade and Plantations were fo folicitous to afcertain the territory of the Six Nations, that Dr. Mitchel, by their defire, publifhed a large map

map of North America; and Mr. Pownal, the prefent Secretary of the Board of Trade, *then* certified, as appears on the map,—That,

for the purpofe from that Board.—In this map Dr. Mitchel obferves, ' That the Six ' Nations have extended their territories, ever ' fince the year 1672, *when they fubdued and* ' *were incorporated with the antient Shawaneffe,* ' *the native proprietors of thefe countries, and* ' *the river Ohio:* befides which, they like- ' wife claim a right of conqueft over the ' Illinois, and all the Miffiffippi, as far as they ' extend. This,' he adds, ' is confirmed by ' their own claims and poffeffions in 1742, ' which include all the bounds here laid ' down, and none have ever thought fit to ' difpute them.' And, in confirmation of this right of the Six Nations to the country on the Ohio, as mentioned by the King's minifters, in their memorial to the Duke of Mirepoix in 1755, we would juft remark, that the Six Nations, Shawaneffe and Delawares, were in the *actual occupation* of the lands *fouthward* of the Great Kenhawa for fome time after the French had encroached
upon

upon the river Ohio; and that in the year 1752, these tribes had a large town on Kentucke river,—238 miles below the *Sioto*:— that in the year 1754, they resided and hunted on the *southerly* side of the river Ohio, in the *Low Country*, at about 320 miles *below* the Great Kenbawa;—and in the year 1755, they had also a large town opposite to the mouth of Sioto;—*at the very place* which is the *southern boundary* line of the tract of land applied for by Mr. Walpole and his associates.—But it is a certain fact, that the Cherokees *never* had any towns or settlements in the country *southward* of the Great Kenhawa;—that they do *not* hunt there, and that neither the Six Nations, Shawanesse nor Delawares, do *now* reside or hunt on the southerly side of the river Ohio, nor did *not* for several years *before* they sold the country to the King. These are facts which can be easily and fully proved.

" In October 1768, at a congress held with the Six Nations at Fort Stanwix, they observed to Sir William Johnson: " Now, bro-
' ther, you who know all our affairs, must be
' sensible

' sensible that *our* rights go much farther
' to the *southward* than the *Kenhawa*,—and
' that we have a very good and clear title
' as far *south* as the *Cherokee river*, which we
' cannot allow to be the right of any other
' Indians, without doing wrong to our poste-
' rity, and acting unworthy those warriors
' who fought and conquered it;—we there-
' fore expect this our right will be con-
' sidered.'

" In November 1768, the Six Nations sold to the King all the country on the southerly side of the river Ohio, as far as to the Cherokee river; but notwithstanding that sale, as soon as it was understood in Virginia that government *favoured* the pretensions of the Cherokees, and that Dr. Walker and Colonel Lewis (the commissioners sent from that colony to the congress at Fort Stanwix) had returned from thence, the late Lord Bottetourt sent these gentlemen to Charles-town, South Carolina, to endeavour to convince Mr. Stuart, the Southern Superintendant of Indian affairs, of the necessity of enlarging the boundary line, which he had settled with the
Chero-

Cherokees;—and to run it from the *Great Kenhawa* to Holston's river. These gentlemen were appointed commissioners by his Lordship, as they had been long conversant in Indian affairs, and were well acquainted with the actual extent of the Cherokee country. Whilst these commissioners were in South Carolina, they wrote a letter to Mr. Stuart, as he had been but a very few years in the Indian service, (and could not, from the nature of his former employment, be supposed to be properly informed about the Cherokee territory,) respecting the claims of the Cherokees to the lands *southward* of the Great Kenbawa, and therein they expressed themselves as follows:

'Charles-town, South Carolina,
Feb. 2, 1769.

' The country *southward* of *the Big Ken-*
' *hawa was never claimed by the Cherokees*,
' and now is the property of the Crown, as
' Sir William Johnson purchased it of the
' Six Nations at a very considerable expence,
' and took a deed of cession from them at Fort
' Stanwix.'

" In

" In 1769, the House of Burgesses of the colony of Virginia represented to Lord Bottetourt, ' That they have the greatest reason ' to fear the said line,' (meaning the boundary line, which the Lords Commissioners for Trade and Plantations have referred to in the map annexed to their Lordships' report,) ' if confirmed, would constantly open to the ' Indians, and others *enemies* to his Majesty, ' a free and easy ingress to the heart of the ' country on the Ohio, Holston's river, and ' the Great Kenhawa; whereby the settle- ' ments which may be attempted in these ' quarters, will, in all probability, be utterly ' destroyed, and *that great extent of country* ' [at least 800 miles in length] *from the mouth* ' *of the Kenhawa* to the *mouth of the Che-* ' *rokee river* extending eastward as far as the ' Laurell Hill, *so lately ceded to his Majesty,* ' *to which no tribe of Indians at present set* ' *up any pretensions, will be entirely aban-* ' *doned to the Cherokees;* in consequence of ' which, claims, *totally destructive* of the true ' interest of his Majesty, may at some future ' time arise, *and acquisitions justly ranked among* ' *the most valuable of the late war be alto-* ' *gether lost.*'

" From

" From the foregoing detail of facts, it is obvious,

" 1st, That the country *southward* of the *Great Kenhawa*, at least as far as the Cherokee river, originally belonged to the Shawaneffe.

" 2d, That the Six Nations, in virtue of their conquest of the Shawaneffe, became the lawful proprietors of that country.

" 3d, That the King, in consequence of the grant from the Six Nations, made to his Majesty at Fort Stanwix in 1768, is *now* vested with the undoubted right and property thereof.

" 4th, That the Cherokees *never* resided nor hunted in that country, and have *not* any kind of right to it.

" 5th, That the House of Burgesses of the colony of Virginia have, upon good grounds, afferted, [such as properly arise from the nature of their stations, and proximity to the Cherokee country,] that the Cherokees had
not

not any juſt pretenſions to the territory *ſouth-ward* of the Great Kenbawa.

" And laſtly, That neither the Six Nations, the Shawaneſſe nor Delawares, do *now* reſide, or hunt in that country.

" From theſe conſiderations, it is evident no poſſible injury can ariſe to his Majeſty's ſervice,—to the Six Nations and their confederacy,—or to the Cherokees, by permitting us to ſettle the *whole* of the lands comprehended within our contract with the Lords Commiſſioners of the Treaſury:——If, however, there has been any treaty held with the Six Nations, *ſince* the ceſſion made to his Majeſty at Fort Stanwix, whereby the faith of the crown is pledged, both to the Six Nations and the Cherokees, that no ſettlements ſhould be made beyond the line, marked on their Lordſhips' report; we ſay, if ſuch agreement has been made by the orders of government with theſe tribes, (notwithſtanding, as the Lords Commiſſioners have acknowledged, '*the Six Nations had ceded the property in the lands to his Majeſty*')—We flatter ourselves, that the objection of their Lordships in the second paragraph of their Report, will be entirely obviated by a specific clause being inserted in the King's grant to us, *expressly prohibiting us from settling any part of the same*, until such time as we shall have *first* obtained his Majesty's allowance, and the full consent of the Cherokees, and the Six Nations and their confederates, for that purpose.

" III. In regard to the third paragraph *principle* of the Board of Trade, *after* the treaty of Paris, ' to *confine* the western extent ' of settlements to such a distance from the ' sea-coast, as that these settlements should ' lie within the *reach* of the trade and com- ' merce of this kingdom,' &c. we shall not presume to controvert;—but it may be observed, that the settlement of the country, *over* the Allegany mountains, and on the Ohio, was *not* understood, either *before* the treaty of Paris, nor intended to be so considered by his Majesty's proclamation of October 1763, ' as *without the reach of the trade and com-*
' *merce*

'*merce of this kingdom,*' &c.;—for, in the year 1748, Mr. John Hanbury, and a number of other gentlemen, petitioned the King for a grant of 500,000 acres of land *over* the Allegany mountains, and on the river Ohio and its branches; and the Lords Commissioners for Trade and Plantations were *then* pleased to *report* to the Lords Committee of his Majesty's most honourable Privy Council, '*That the settlement of the country, lying to the westward* of the *great mountains,* as it was the centre of the British dominions, *would be for his Majesty's interest,* and the advantage and security of Virginia and the neighbouring colonies.'

" And on the 23d of February 1748-9, the Lords Commissioners for Trade and Plantations *again reported* to the Lords of the Committee of the Privy Council, that they had '*fully set forth the great utility and advantage of extending our settlements beyond the great mountains* (which *Report has been approved of by your Lordships*).—And as, by these *new* proposals, there is *a great probability of having a much larger tract of*

' *the said country settled than under the former,*
' *we are of opinion, that it will be greatly for*
' *his Majesty's service,* and '*the welfare and*
' *security of Virginia, to comply with the prayer*
' *of the petition.*'

" And on the 16th of March 1748-9, an *instruction* was sent to the Governor of Virginia to grant 500,000 acres of land *over the Allegany mountains* to the aforesaid Mr. Hanbury and his partners (who are now *part* of the company of Mr. Walpole and his associates); and that instruction sets forth, That
' *such settlements will be for our interest,* and
' the *advantage* and *security of our said colony,*
' *as well as the advantage of the neighbouring*
' *ones;—*inasmuch as our loving subjects *will*
' *be thereby enabled to cultivate a friendship,*
' *and carry on a more extensive commerce* with
' the nations of Indians inhabiting those
' parts; *and such examples may likewise induce*
' *the neighbouring colonies to turn their thoughts*
' *towards designs of the same nature.*'——
Hence we apprehend, it is evident, that a former Board of Trade, at which Lord Halifax presided, was of opinion, that settlements
over

over the Allegany mountains were not against the King's interest, *nor* at such a distance from the sea-coast, as to *be without* 'the *reach* ' of the trade and commerce of this king- ' dom,' nor *where* its authority or juris- diction could not be exercised.—But the *Report* under consideration suggests, that two capital objects of the proclamation of 1763 were, *to confine* ' future settlements to the ' sources of the rivers which fall into the sea ' from the west and north-west,' (or, in other words, to *the eastern side of the Allegany mountains,*) and to the three new governments of Canada, East Florida, and West Florida;— and to establish this fact, the Lords Commissioners for Trade and Plantations recite a part of that proclamation.

" But if the *whole* of this proclamation is considered, it will be found to contain the nine following heads: *viz.*

" 1st, To declare to his Majesty's subjects, that he had erected four distinct and separate governments in America; *viz.* Quebec, East Florida, West Florida, and Grenada.

" 2d, To

"2d, To ascertain the respective boundaries of these four new governments.

" 3d, To testify the royal sense and approbation of the conduct and bravery, both of the officers and soldiers of the King's army, and of the reduced officers of the navy, who had served in North America, and to reward them by grants of lands in Quebec, and in East and West Florida, without fee or reward:

" 4th, To hinder the Governors of Quebec, East Florida and West Florida, from granting warrants of survey, or passing patents for lands, *beyond* the bounds of their respective governments.

" 5th, To forbid the governors of any other colonies or plantations in America, from granting warrants or passing patents for lands, *beyond* the heads or sources of any of the rivers, which fall into the Atlantic Ocean from the west or north-west, or upon any lands whatever, ' *which, not having been* ' CEDED *to or purchased by the King,* are
' reserved

‘ referved to the faid Indians, or any of
‘ them.’

" 6th, To referve, '*for the prefent*,' under the King's fovereignty, protection, and dominion, *for the ufe of the faid Indians*, all the lands *not* included within the limits of the faid three new governments, or within the limits of the Hudfon's Bay Company; as alfo, all the lands lying to the weftward of the fources of the rivers, which fall into the fea from the weft and north-weft, and forbidding the King's fubjects from making any purchafes of fettlements whatever, or taking poffeffion of the lands *fo referved*, without his Majefty's leave and licence firft obtained.

" 7th, To require all perfons, who had made fettlements on lands, *not* purchafed by the King from the Indians, to remove from fuch fettlements.

" 8th, To regulate the future purchafes of lands from the Indians, within fuch parts as his Majesty, by that proclamation, permitted settlements to be made.

"9th, To declare, that the trade with the Indians should be free and open to all his Majesty's subjects, and to prescribe the manner how it shall be carried on.

"And lastly, To require all military officers, and the superintendants of Indian affairs, to seize and apprehend all persons who stood charged with treasons, murders, &c. and who had fled from justice, and taken refuge in the reserved lands of the Indians, to send such persons to the colony, *where* they stood accused.

"From this proclamation, therefore, it is obvious, that the sole design of it, independent of the establishment of the three new governments, ascertaining their respective boundaries, rewarding the officers and soldiers, and regulating the Indian trade, and apprehending felons, was to *convince* the Indians 'of his Majesty's justice and determined 'reso-

'resolution to remove all reasonable cause of 'discontent,' by interdicting all settlements on land, not *ceded to or purchased by his Majesty;* and declaring it to be, as we have already mentioned, his royal will and pleasure, ' for *the present, to reserve,* under his so- ' vereignty, protection, and dominion, *for* ' *the use of the Indians,* all the lands and ' territories lying to the westward of the ' sources of the rivers which fall into the ' sea from the west and north-west.'—Can any words express more decisively the royal intention?—Do they not explicitly mention, That the territory is, *at present,* reserved under his Majesty's protection, *for the use of the Indians?*—And as the Indians had *no use* for those lands, which are bounded *westerly* by the *south-east side* of the river Ohio, either for residence or hunting, they were willing to sell them; and accordingly did sell them to the King in November 1768, (the occasion of which sale will be fully explained in our observations in the succeeding paragraphs of the *Report).*—Of course, the proclamation, so far as it regarded the settlement of the lands included within that purchase, has ab-

solutely

solutely and undoubtedly ceased.—The late Mr. Grenville, who was, at the time of issuing this proclamation, the minister of this kingdom, always admitted, that the design of it was totally accomplished, *so soon as the country was purchased of the natives.*

" IV. In this paragraph, the Lords Commissioners for Trade and Plantations mention two reasons for his Majesty's entering into engagements with the Indians, for fixing a *more precise and determinate boundary line* than was settled by the proclamation of October 1763, *viz.*

" 1st, Partly for want of *precision* in the one intended to be marked by the proclamation of 1763.

" 2d, And partly from a consideration of justice in regard to *legal titles to lands.*

" We have, we presume, fully proved, in our observations on the third paragraph, That the design of the proclamation; so far as it related to lands *westward* of the Allegany

gany mountains, was for no other purpose than to *reserve* them, under his Majesty's protection, for *the present, for the use of the Indians;* to which we shall only add, That the line established by the proclamation, so far as it concerned the lands in question, could *not* possibly be fixed and described with more *precision*, than the proclamation itself describes it; for it declares, That ' all the lands and
' territories lying to the westward of the
' sources of the rivers, *which fall into the*
' *sea from the west and north-west*,' should be reserved under his Majesty's protection.

" Neither, in our opinion, was his Majesty induced to enter into engagements with the Indians for fixing a more *precise* and determinate boundary ' *partly from a consideration*
' *of justice, in regard to legal titles to lands*,'
—for there were *none* such (as we shall prove) comprehended within the tract *now* under consideration.

" But for a full comprehension of ALL the reasons for his Majesty's ' entering into en-
' gagements with the Indians, for fixing a
' more

'more precise and determinate boundary line' than was settled by the royal proclamation of October 1763, we shall take the liberty of stating the following facts:—In the year 1764, the King's ministers had it *then* in contemplation to obtain an act of parliament for the proper regulation of the Indian commerce; and providing a fund (by laying a duty on the trade) for the support of superintendants, commissaries, interpreters, &c. at particular forts in the Indian country, *where* the trade was to be carried on:—And as a part of this system, it was thought proper, in order to avoid future complaints from the Indians, on account of encroachments on their hunting-grounds, to purchase a large tract of territory from them, and establish, with their consent, a respectable *boundary line*, beyond which his Majesty's subjects should *not* be permitted to settle.

" In consequence of this system, orders were transmitted to Sir William Johnson, in the year 1764, to call together the Six Nations, lay this proposition of the *boundary* before them, and take their opinion upon it.—This,

This, we apprehend, will appear evident from the following speech, made by Sir William to the Six Nations, at a conference which he held with them, at Johnson Hall, May the 2d, 1765.

' Brethren,
' The last but the most important affair I
' have at this time to mention, is with regard
' to the *settling a boundary between you and*
' *the English*. I sent a message to some
' of your nations some time ago, to acquaint
' you, that I should confer with you at this
' meeting upon it. The King, whose ge-
' nerosity and forgiveness you have already
' experienced, *being very desirous to put a*
' *final end to disputes between his people and*
' YOU CONCERNING LANDS, and to do you
' strict justice, has fallen upon the plan of
' a boundary between our provinces and the
' Indians (which no white man shall dare
' to invade) as the best and surest method of
' ending such like disputes, and *securing*
' *your property* to you, beyond a possibility
' of disturbance. This will, I hope, appear
' to you so reasonable, so just on the part
' of

' of the King, and so advantageous to you
' and your posterity, that I can have no
' doubt of your chearfully joining with me
' in settling such a division-line, as will
' be best for the advantage of both white
' men and Indians, *and as shall best agree*
' *with the extent and increase of each pro-*
' *vince,* and the governors, whom I shall
' consult upon that occasion, so soon as I am
' fully empowered; but in the mean time
' I am desirous to know in what manner you
' would choose to extend it, and what you
' will heartily agree to, and abide by, in
' general terms. At the same time I am
' to acquaint you, that whenever the whole
' is settled, and that it shall appear you have
' *so far consulted the increasing state of our*
' *people, as to make any convenient cessions of*
' *ground* where it is most wanted, that *then*
' you will receive a considerable present in
' return for your friendship.'

"To this speech the Sachems and Warriors of the Six Nations, after conferring some time among themselves, gave an answer to Sir William Johnson, and agreed to the proposition

position of the boundary line;—which answer, and the other transactions of this conference, Sir William transmitted to the office of the Lords Commissioners for Trade and Plantations.

" From a change of the administration, which formed the above system of obtaining an act of parliament for regulating the Indian trade, and establishing the *boundary line,* or from some other public cause, unknown to us,—no measures were adopted, until the latter end of the year 1767, for *completing* the negotiation about this boundary line.— But in the mean time, *viz.* between the years 1765 and 1768, the King's subjects removed in *great* numbers from Virginia, Maryland, and Pennsylvania, and settled *over* the mountains,—upon which account, the Six Nations became so irritated, that in the year 1766 they killed several persons, and denounced a general war against the middle colonies; and to appease them, and to avoid such a public calamity, a detachment of the 42d regiment of foot was *that year* sent from the garrison of Fort Pitt, to remove such settlers

as were feated at *Red Stone Creek*, &c.—but the endeavours and threats of that detachment proved ineffectual, and they returned to the garrifon, without being able to execute their orders.—The complaints of the Six Nations however continuing and *increafing*, on account of the fettling of their lands over the mountains, General Gage wrote to the Governor of Pennfylvania on the 7th of December 1767, and after mentioning thefe complaints, he obferved, ' *You are a wit-*
' *nefs how little attention has been paid to the*
' *feveral proclamations that have been pub-*
' *lifhed; and that even the removing thofe*
' *people from the lands in queftion*, which *was*
' *attempted this fummer by the garrifon at*
' *Fort Pitt*, has *been only a temporary expe-*
' *dient.* We learn they are *returned again*
' to the fame *encroachments* on Red Stone
' Creek and Cheat River in *greater numbers*
' *than ever.*'

" On the 5th of January 1768, the Governor of Pennfylvania fent a meffage to the General Affembly of the province with the foregoing letter from General Gage;—and on
the

the 13th the Assembly, in the conclusion of a message to the Governor on the subject of Indian complaints, observed, ' To obviate
' which cause of their discontent, and ef-
' fectually to establish between them and his
' Majesty's subjects a durable peace, we are
' of opinion, that a speedy *confirmation* of the
' *boundary*, and a just satisfaction made to
' them for their lands on this side of it, are
' absolutely necessary. By this means all
' their present complaints of encroachments
' will be removed, and the people on our
' frontiers will have a sufficient country *to*
' *settle or hunt in, without interfering with*
' *them*.'

" On the 19th of January 1768, Mr. Galloway, the Speaker of the Assembly in Pennsylvania, and the Committee of Correspondence, wrote on the subject of the Indians disquietude, by order of the House, to their agents Richard Jackson and Benjamin Franklin, Esquires, in London; and therein they said, ' That the delay of the confirmation of
' the *boundary* the natives have warmly com-
' plained of, *and that although they have re-*
' *ceived*

'*ceived no consideration* for the *lands agreed*
'*to be ceded to the crown on our* side of the
' boundary, *yet that its subjects are daily set-*
' *tling and occupying those very lands.*'

"In April 1768, the legislature of Pennsylvania finding that the expectations of an Indian war were hourly increasing, *occasioned by the settlement of the lands over the mountains*, not sold by the natives; and flattering themselves, that orders would soon arrive from England for the perfection of the boundary line; they voted the sum of one thousand pounds, to be given as a present, in blankets, strouds, &c. to the Indians upon the Ohio, with a view of moderating their resentment, until these orders should arrive: and the Governor of Pennsylvania being informed, that a treaty was soon to be held at Fort Pitt by George Croghan Esq. deputy agent of Indian affairs, by order of General Gage and Sir William Johnson, he sent his secretary and another gentleman, as commissioners from the province, to deliver the above present to the Indians at Fort Pitt.

" On

" On the 2d of May 1768, the Six Nations made the following speech at that conference:

' BROTHER,
' It is not without grief that we see our
' country *settled by you*, without our know-
' ledge or consent; and it is a long time since
' we complained to you of this grievance,
' which we find has not yet been redressed;
' but *settlements* are still *extending further*
' *into our country:* some of them are made
' directly on our war-path, leading to our
' enemies country, and we do not like it.
' Brother, you have *laws among you* to govern
' your people by; and it will be the strongest
' proof of the sincerity of your friendship,
' to let us see that you remove the people
' from our lands; as we look upon it, *they*
' *will have time enough to settle them, when*
' *you have purchased them, and the country*
' *becomes yours.*'

" The Pennsylvania commissioners, in answer to this speech, informed the Six Nations, that the Governor of that province had sent

four

four gentlemen with his proclamation and the act of assembly (making it *felony of death* without benefit of clergy, to continue on Indian lands) to such settlers *over* the mountains as were seated within the limits of Pennsylvania, requiring them to vacate their settlements; but all to no avail:—that the Governor of Virginia had likewise, to as little purpose, issued his proclamations and orders, and that General Gage had twice *ineffectually* sent parties of soldiers to remove the settlers from Red Stone Creek and Monongehela.

" As soon as Mr. Jackson and Dr. Franklin received the foregoing instructions from the General Assembly of Pennsylvania, they waited upon the American minister, and urged the expediency and necessity of the boundary line being speedily concluded; and, in consequence thereof, additional orders were immediately transmitted to Sir William Johnson for that purpose.

" It is plain, therefore, that the proclamation of October 1763 was *not* designed, as the

the Lords Commissioners for Trade and Plantations have suggested, to signify the policy of this kingdom, *against* settlements *over* the Allegany mountains, *after* the King had actually purchased the territory; and that the *true* reasons for purchasing the lands comprised within that boundary were to avoid an Indian rupture, and give an opportunity to the King's subjects quietly and lawfully to settle thereon.

" V. Whether the Lords Commissioners for Trade and Plantations are well founded in their declarations, that the lands under consideration ' *are out of all advantageous in-* ' *tercourse with this kingdom*,' shall be fully considered in our observations on the sixth paragraph :—and as to ' the various propo- ' sitions for erecting new colonies in the ' *interior parts*, which, their Lordships say, ' have been, in consequence of the extension ' of the boundary line, submitted to the ' consideration of government, particularly ' in *that part of the country* wherein are situ- ' ated the lands now prayed for, and the ' danger of complying with such proposals 'have been so obvious, as to *defeat* every attempt for carrying them into execution;'—we shall only observe on this paragraph, that as we do not know what these propositions were, or upon what principle the proposers have been *defeated*, it is impossible for us to judge, whether they are any ways applicable to our case.—Consistent however with our knowledge, no more than one proposition, for the settlement of a *part* of the lands in question, has been presented to government; and that was from Dr. Lee, 32 other Americans, and two Londoners, in the year 1768; praying that his Majesty would *grant* to them, without *any purchase-money*, 2,500,000 acres of land *in one or more surveys*, to be located between the 38th and 42d degrees of latitude, *over the Allegany mountains*, and on condition of their possessing these lands 12 *years* WITHOUT *the payment of any quit-rent* (the same *not* to begin until the whole 2,500,000 acres were surveyed); and that they should be obliged to settle only 200 *families in* 12 *years*. Surely, the Lords Commissioners did not mean this proposition as one that was similar, and

and would *apply* to the cafe now *reported* upon; and efpecially as Dr. Lee and his affociates did not propofe, as we do, either to purchafe the lands, or pay the quit-rents to his Majefty, *neat and clear of all deductions*, or be at the *whole* expence of eftablifhing and maintaining the civil government of the country.

" VI. In the fixth paragraph the Lords Commiffioners obferve, That ' *every argument* ' *on the fubject*, refpecting the fettlement of ' the lands in that part of the country now ' prayed for, *is collected together, with great* ' *force and precifion, in a Reprefentation made* ' *to his Majefty* by the Lords Commiffioners ' for Trade and Plantations, in March 1768.'

" That it may be clearly underftood what was the occafion of this *Reprefentation*, we fhall take the liberty of mentioning, that on the 1ft of October 1767, and during the time that the Earl of Shelburne was Secretary of State for the fouthern department, an idea was entertained of forming, ' *at the expence* ' *of the crown*,' three *new governments* in

North America, *viz.* one at *Detroit* [on the waters between Lake Huron and Lake Erie]; one in the *Illinois Country*, and one on the *lower* part of the river Ohio: and in confequence of fuch an idea, a *reference* was made by his Lordfhip to the Lords Commiffioners for Trade and Plantations, for their opinion upon thefe propofed *new* governments.

" Having plainly explained the caufe of the *Reprefentation*, which is fo very ftrongly and earneftly infifted upon by the Lords Commiffioners for Trade and Plantations, as containing ' *every argument on the fubject* of ' the lands which is at prefent before your ' Lordfhips;' we fhall now give our reafons for apprehending, *that it* is fo far from applying againft our cafe, that it actually declares a permiffion would be given to fettle the very lands in queftion.

" Three principal reafons are affigned in the *Reprefentation*, ' as conducive to the great ' object of colonizing upon the continent of ' North America', *viz.*

" 1ft,

" 1ſt, ' Promoting the advantageous fiſhery
' carried on upon the *northern coaſt*.'

" 2dly, ' Encouraging the growth and cul-
' ture of naval ſtores, and of *raw materials*,
' to be tranſported hither, in exchange for
' perfect manufactures and other merchan-
' dize.'

" 3dly, ' Securing a ſupply of lumber, pro-
' viſions, and other neceſſaries, for the ſup-
' port of our eſtabliſhments in the American
' iſlands.'

" On the firſt of theſe reaſons, we apprehend, it is not neceſſary for us to make many
obſervations; as the provinces of New Jerſey,
Pennſylvania, Maryland, and Virginia, and
the colonies *ſouthward* of them, have *not*, and
from the nature of their ſituation and commerce will *not*, promote the *fiſhery* more, it
is conceived, than the propoſed Ohio colony.
Theſe provinces are, however, beneficial
to this kingdom, in the culture and exportation of different articles;—as it is humbly
preſumed the 'Ohio colony *will* likewiſe be,

if the production *of staple commodities* is allowed to be within that description.

" On the 2d and 3d general reasons of the *Representation* we shall observe, that no part of his Majesty's dominions in North America will require less *encouragement* ' for the growth ' and culture of naval stores and raw mate-' ' rials, and for the supplying the islands ' with lumber, provisions,' &c. than the solicited colony on the Ohio;—and for the following reasons:

" First; The lands in question are excellent, the climate temperate, the native grapes, silk-worms, and mulberry-trees, are every where; hemp grows spontaneously in the valleys and low lands; iron-ore is plenty in the hills; and no soil is better adapted for the culture of tobacco, flax, and cotton, than that of the Ohio.

" Second; The country is well watered by several navigable rivers, communicating with each other; and by which, and a short land-carriage of *only* 40 *miles*, the produce of the
lands

lands of the Ohio can, even *now*, be fent *cheaper* to the fea-port town of Alexandria, on the river Potomack, (where General Braddock's tranfports landed his troops,) than any kind of merchandize is at this time fent *from Northampton to London*.

" Third; The rivér Ohio is, at *all* feafons of the year, navigable for large boats, like the Weft Country barges, rowed only by four or five men; and from the month of January to the month of April, large fhips may be built on the Ohio, and fent laden with *hemp, iron, flax, filk*, &c. to this kingdom.

" Fourth; Flour, corn, beef, fhip-plank, and other neceffaries, can be fent down the ftream of the Ohio to Weft Florida, and from thence to the iflands, much cheaper, and in better order, than from New York or Philadelphia.

" Fifth; Hemp, tobacco, iron, and fuch bulky articles, can alfo be fent *down* the *ftream* of the Ohio to the *fea*, at-leaft 50 *per centum* cheaper than thefe articles were ever

ever carried by a land carriage, of only 60 miles, in Pennſylvania,—where *waggonage* is cheaper than in any other part of North America.

" Sixth; The expence of tranſporting Britiſh manufactories from the ſea to the Ohio colony will *not* be ſo much as is now paid, and muſt ever be paid, to a great part of the countries of *Pennſylvania, Virginia,* and *Maryland.*

" From this ſtate of facts, we apprehend, it is clear that the lands in queſtion are altogether capable, and will advantageouſly admit, from their fertility, ſituation, and the ſmall expence attending the exporting the produce of them to this kingdom,—' of *conducing* ' to the great object of colonizing upon ' the continent of North America:'—but that we may more particularly elucidate this important point, we ſhall take the freedom of obſerving,—that it is *not* diſputed, but even acknowledged, by the very *Report* now under conſideration, that the climate and ſoil of the Ohio are as favourable as we have deſcribed

described them ;—and as to the native silk-worms, it is a truth, that *above* 10,000 weight of cocoons was, in August 1771, sold at the public filature in Philadelphia ;—and that the silk produced from the *native* worm is of a good quality, and has been much approved of in this city.—As to *hemp*, we are ready to make it appear, that it grows, as we have represented, spontaneously, and of a good texture on the Ohio.—When, therefore, the *increasing* dependence of this kingdom upon *Russia*, for this very article, is considered, and that none has been exported from the *sea-coast American colonies*, as their soil will not easily produce it,—this dependence must surely be admitted as a subject of great national consequence, and worthy of the serious attention of government. Nature has pointed out to us *where* any quantity of hemp can be soon and easily raised; and by that means, not only a large amount of specie may be retained *yearly* in this kingdom, but our own subjects can be employed most advantageously, and paid in the *manufactures* of this kingdom. The state of the Russian trade is briefly thus:

From

From the year 1722 to 1731, —250 ſhips were, on a medium, ſent each year to St. Peterſburgh, Narva, Riga, and Archangel, for *hemp*,   250 ſhips.

And from the year 1762 to 1771,—500 ſhips were alſo ſent for that purpoſe,   500
_____
Increaſe in ten years,   250 ſhips.

" Here, then, it is obvious that in the laſt *ten* years there was, on a medium, an increaſe of 250 ſhips in the Ruſſian trade. Can it be conſiſtent with the wiſdom and policy of the greateſt naval and commercial nation in the world, to depend wholly on *foreigners* for the ſupply of an article, in which is included the very exiſtence of her navy and commerce? Surely not; and eſpecially when God has bleſſed us with a country yielding *naturally* the very commodity which draws our money from us, and renders us *dependent* on Ruſſia for it.

" As we have only hitherto *generally* ſtated the *ſmall* expence of carriage between the

waters

waters of Potomack and thofe of the Ohio, we fhall now endeavour to fhew how very ill founded the Lords for Trade and Plantations are, in the fifth paragraph of their *Report*, viz. That the lands in queftion ' are ' *out of all advantageous intercourfe with this* ' *kingdom.*' In order, however, that a proper opinion may be formed on this important article, we fhall take the liberty of ftating the particular expence of carriage, *even during* the laft *French war*, (when there was no *back* carriage from the Ohio to Alexandria,) as it will be found, it was even *then* only about a *halfpenny* per *pound*, as will appear from the following account, the truth of which we fhall fully afcertain, *viz.*

	£. s. d.	
From Alexandria to Fort Cumberland, by water,	0 1 7	*per cwt.*
From Fort Cumberland to Redftone Creek, at 14 dollars *per* waggon-load, each waggon carrying 15 *cwt*, -	0 4 2	
	0 5 9	

Note—

Note—The distance was *then* 70 miles, but by a *new* waggon-road, *lately* made, it is *now* but forty miles—a saving, of course, of above one-half the 5*s.* 9*d.* is *at present* experienced.

" If it is considered that this rate of carriage was *in time of war,* and *when* there were no inhabitants on the Ohio, we cannot doubt but every intelligent mind will be satisfied, that it is now much *less* than is daily paid in London for the carriage of *coarse woollens, cutlery, iron ware,* &c. from several counties in England.

The following is the Cost of Carriage from Birmingham, &c. viz.

From Birmingham to London, is 4*s. per cwt.*
From Walsall in Staffordshire, 5*s.*
From Sheffield, 8*s.*
From Warrington, 7*s.*

" If the lands which are at present under consideration, are, as the Lords Commissioners for Trade and Plantations say, ' *out of all ad-* ' *vantageous intercourse with this kingdom,*'
we

we are at a loss to conceive by what standard that Board calculates the rate of ' advan-
' tageous intercourse.'—If the King's sub-
jects, settled *over* the Allegany mountains, and on the Ohio, within the *new*-erected county of Bedford, in the province of Penn-
sylvania, are altogether cloathed with British manufacture, as is the case; is that country ' out of all advantageous intercourse with ' this kingdom?'—If merchants in London are *now* actually shipping British manufactures for the use *of the very settlers* on the lands in question, does that exportation come within the Lords Commissioners description of what is ' out of all advantageous inter-
' course with this kingdom?' In short, the Lords Commissioners admit, upon their own principles, that it is a political and advan-
tageous intercourse with this kingdom, *when* the settlements and settlers are confined to the *eastern* side of the Allegany mountains. Shall then the expence of carriage, even of the very coarsest and heaviest cloths, or other articles, from the *mountains* to the Ohio, only about 70 miles, and which will not, at most, *increase* the price of carriage *above a halfpenny*

a yard, convert the trade and connexion with the settlers on the Ohio, into a predicament ' that shall be, as the Lords Commissioners ' have said, *out* of all advantageous inter' course with this kingdom?'—On the whole, ' if the poor Indians in the remote parts of ' North America are *now* able to pay for ' the linens, woollens, and iron ware, they ' are furnished with by English traders, ' though Indians have nothing but what ' they get by hunting, and the goods are ' loaded with all the impositions fraud and ' knavery can contrive, to *inhance* their value; ' will not industrious English farmers,' employed in the culture of hemp, flax, silk, *&c.* ' be able to pay for what shall be brought ' to them in the fair way of commerce;' and especially when it is remembered, that there is *no other allowable* market for the sale of these articles than in this kingdom?— And if, ' the growths of *the* country find ' their way out of it, will not the manu' factures of this kingdom, *where* the ' hemp, *&c.* must be sent to, find their way ' into it?'

" Whether

"Whether Nova Scotia, and East and West Florida have yielded advantages and returns equal to the enormous sums expended in founding and supporting them, or even advantages, such as the Lords' Commissioners for Trade and Plantations, in their *Representation* of 1768, seemed to expect, it is not our business to investigate:—it is, we presume, sufficient for us to mention, that those 'many principal persons in Pennsylvania,' as is observed in the *Representation*, 'whose names and association lie before your Majesty in Council, for the purpose of making settlements in Nova Scotia,' have, several years since, been convinced of the impracticability of exciting settlers to move from the *middle colonies*, and settle in that province; and even of those who were prevailed on to go to Nova Scotia, the greater part of them returned with great complaints against the severity and length of the winters.

"As to East and West Florida, it is, we are persuaded, morally impossible to *force* the people of the *middle* provinces, between 37 and 40 degrees north latitude, (where there

is plenty of vacant land in their own temperate climate,) to remove to the scorching, unwholesome heats of these provinces. The inhabitants of Montpelier might as soon and as easily be persuaded to remove to the northern parts of Russia, or to Senegal.—In short, it is contending with nature, and the experience of all ages, to attempt to compel a people, *born* and *living in a temperate climate*, and in the neighbourhood of a rich, healthful, and uncultivated country, to travel several hundred miles to a *sea-port* in order to make a *voyage to sea;* and settle either in extreme hot or cold latitudes. If the county of York was vacant and uncultivated, and the more *southern* inhabitants of this island were in want of land, would they suffer themselves to be driven to the *north of Scotland?*—Would they not, in spite of all opposition, *first* possess themselves of that fertile country?—Thus much we have thought necessary to remark, in respect to the general principles laid down in the *Representation* of 1768; and we hope we have shewn, that the arguments *therein* made use of, do *not* in any degree militate against the subject in question;
but

but that they were intended, and do solely apply to ' new colonies proposed to be estab-
' lished,' as the *Representation* says, ' *at an*
' *expence to this kingdom*,' at the distance of
' above 1500 miles from the sea, which from
' their inability to find returns, *wherewith*
' to pay for the manufactures of Great Bri-
' tain, will be probably led to manufacture
' for themselves, *as they would*,' continues
the *Representation*, ' be separated from the *old*
' colonies by immense tracts of unpeopled
' desart.'—

" It now only remains for us to inquire, whether it was the intention of the Lords Commissioners for Trade and Plantations in 1768, that the territory, which would be included within the *boundary line*, then negociating with the Indians, (and which was the *one* that was *that year* perfected,) should continue a useless wilderness, or be settled and occupied by his Majesty's subjects.—The very *Representation* itself, which the present Lords Commissioners for Trade and Plantations say contains ' *every argument on the*
' *subject*,' furnishes us an ample and satisfac-
tory

tory folution to this important queftion.—The Lords Commiffioners in 1768, after pronouncing their opinion *againft* the *propofed three new governments*, as above ftated, declare, 'They ought to be carefully guarded
'againft, by encouraging the fettlement of
'that extenfive tract of fea-coaft hitherto
'unoccupied; which, fay their Lordfhips,
'*together with the liberty, that the inhabitants*
'OF THE *middle colonies* WILL HAVE (in
'confequence of the propofed *boundary line*
'with the Indians) *of gradually extending,*
'*themfelves backwards*, will *more effectually*
'*and beneficially anfwer* the object of *encou-*
'*raging population* and *confumption*, than the
'erection of new governments; fuch gradual
'extenfion might, through the medium of a
'continual population, upon even the fame
'extent of territory, *preferve* a communi-
'cation of mutual commercial benefits be-
'tween its extremeft parts and Great Britain,
'*impoffible to exift in colonies feparated by im-*
'*menfe tracts of unpeopled defart.*'—Can any opinion be more clear and conclufive, in *favour* of the propofition which we have humbly fubmitted to his Majefty?—for their
Lordfhips

Lordſhips poſitively ſay, that the inhabitants of the middle colonies *will have liberty of gradually extending themſelves backwards;*— but is it not very extraordinary, that after near *two years* deliberation, the preſent Lords Commiſſioners for Trade and Plantations ſhould make a *Report* to the Lords of the Committee of the Privy Council, and therein expreſsly refer to that opinion of 1768, in which, they ſay, ' *every argument on the*
' *ſubject is collected together with great force*
' *and preciſion*,' and yet that, almoſt in the ſame breath, their Lordſhips ' ſhould con-
' travene that very opinion, and adviſe his
' Majeſty *to check the progreſs of their ſettle-*
' *ments?*'—And that ' ſettlements in *that diſ-*
' *tant part* of the country ought to be *diſcou-*
' *raged* as much as poſſible, and another
' proclamation ſhould be iſſued declaratory
' of his Majeſty's reſolution, *not* to allow,
' *for the preſent*, any new ſettlement beyond
' the line;'—to wit, beyond the Allegany mountains?—How ſtrange and contradictory is this conduct?—But we forbear any ſtrictures upon it;—and ſhall conclude our remarks on this head, by ſtating the opinion,

at different times, of the Lords Commissioners for Trade and Plantations on this subject.

" In 1748, their Lordships expressed the strongest desire to promote settlements *over* the mountains and on the Ohio.—

" In 1768—The then Lords Commissioners for Trade and Plantations declared, (in consequence of the boundary line at that time negociating)—That the inhabitants of the *middle colonies* would *have liberty of gradually extending themselves backwards.*

" In 1770—The Earl of Hillsborough actually *recommended* the purchase of a tract of land *over* the mountains, sufficient for a new colony, and then went down to the Lords Commissioners of the Treasury, to know whether their Lordships would treat with Mr. Walpole and his associates, for such purchase.

" In 1772—The Earl of Hillsborough, and the other Lords Commissioners for Trade and Plantations, made a *report* on the petition of Mr.

Mr. Walpole and his associates, and referred to the *Representation* of the Board of Trade in 1768, ' as containing *every argument* on the ' *subject, collected together with force and pre-* ' *cision*'—which *Representation* declared, as we have shewn, ' *That the inhabitants of the* ' *middle colonies* WILL *have liberty to extend* ' *backwards*,' on the identical lands in question; and yet, notwithstanding such *reference*, so strongly made from the present Board of Trade to the opinion of that Board,—the Earl of Hillsborough, and the other Lords Commissioners for Trade and Plantations, have *now*, in direct terms, *reported against* the absolute engagement and opinion of the Board in 1768.

" It may be asked, what was intended by the expressions in the *Representation* of 1768, of *gradually extending themselves backwards?* It is answered, They were only in contradistinction to the proposal of erecting at that time *three new governments at Detroit*, &c. and thereby exciting, as the *Representation* says, the stream of population to *various* distant places.—In short, it was, we think, beyond

yond all doubt, the '*precife*' opinion of the Lords Commiffioners in 1768, That the territory, within the boundary line, then negociating, and fince completed, would be fufficient at that time to anfwer the object of population and confumption; and that until that territory was fully occupied,—it was not neceffary to erect the propofed *three new governments* ' *at an expence to this kingdom,*' in places, as their Lordfhips obferved, ' fepa-
' rated by immenfe tracts of unpeopled de-
' fart.'——

" To conclude our obfervations on the 6th paragraph, we would juft remark,—That we prefume we have demonftrated, that the inhabitants of the middle colonies *cannot* be compelled to *exchange* the foil and climate of thefe colonies, either for the fevere colds of Nova Scotia and Canada, or the unwholefome heats of Eaft and Weft Florida. Let us next enquire, what would be the effect of *confining* thefe inhabitants (if it was practicable) within narrow bounds, and thereby preventing them from exercifing their natural inclination of cultivating lands?—and whether

fuch

such restriction would not force them into *manufactures*, to rival the Mother Country? —To these questions, the Lords Commissioners have, with much candour, replied in their Representation of 1768,—We ' admit,' said their Lordships, ' as an undeniable prin-
' ciple of *true policy*, that, with a view to
' *prevent manufactures*, it is necessary and
' proper *to open* an extent of territory for
' colonization, *proportioned* to an *increase* of
' people, as a large number of inhabitants
' cooped up in narrow limits, without a
' sufficiency of land *for produce*, would be
' compelled to *convert* their attention and
' industry to *manufactures*.'—But their Lordships at the same time observed,—' That the
' *encouragement* given to the settlement of the
' colonies upon the sea-coast, and the effect
' which such encouragement has had, has
' already *effectually* provided for this object.'
In what parts of North America this *encouragement* has thus *provided* for *population*, their Lordships have not mentioned. If the establishment of the governments of Quebec, Nova Scotia, and the Island of St. John's, or East and West Florida, was intended by their
Lordships

Lordships as that effectual provision,—we shall presume to deny the proposition, by asserting, as an undoubted truth,—that although there is at least a *million* of subjects in the middle colonies, none have emigrated from thence, and settled in these *new* provinces;—and for that reason, and from the very nature of colonization itself, we affirm that none *will ever* be induced *to exchange* the healthy, temperate climate of Virginia, Maryland, and Pennsylvania, for the extreme colds or heats of Canada and Nova Scotia, or East and West Florida:—In short, it is not in the power of government to give any encouragement, that can compensate for a desertion of friends and neighbours,—dissolution of family connexions, and abandoning a soil and climate infinitely superior to those of Canada, Nova Scotia, or the Floridas.—Will not, therefore, the inhabitants of the middle provinces, whose population is great beyond example, and who have already made some advances in manufactures, ' by confining ' them to their present narrow limits,' be necessarily compelled to convert their whole attention to that object? How then shall this,

in

in the nature of things, be prevented, except, as the Lords Commissioners have justly remarked, ' by opening an extent of territory ' proportioned *to their increase ?*'—But *where* shall a territory be found proper for ' the ' *colonization* of the inhabitants of the middle ' colonies?' We answer,—in the very country which the Lords Commissioners have said that the inhabitants of these colonies would have liberty to settle in ;—a country which his Majesty has purchased from the Six Nations;—one, *where* several thousands of his subjects are already settled;—and one, *where* the Lords Commissioners have acknowledged, ' a gradual extension might, ' through the medium of a continued po-' pulation, upon even the same extent of ' territory, *preserve a communication* of mu-' tual commercial benefits *between* its *extremest* ' *parts* and Great Britain.'

" VII. This paragraph is introduced, by referring to the extract of a letter from the commander in chief of his Majesty's forces in North America, laid by the Earl of Hillsborough before the Lords Commissioners for

Trade and Plantations;—but as their Lordships have *not* mentioned either the general's name, or the time *when* the letter was written, or what occasioned his delivering his opinion upon the subject of *colonization in general*, in the '*remote countries*,'——we can only conjecture that General Gage was the writer of the letter, and that it was wrote about the year 1768,——*when* the plan of the *three new governments* was under the consideration of the then Lords Commissioners for Trade and Plantations, and *before* the lands on the Ohio were bought from, and the boundary line established with the Six Nations.——Indeed, we think it clear, That the General had *no* other lands at that time under his consideration, than what he calls '*remote countries*,' such as the *Detroit, Illinois,* and the *lower* parts of the Ohio;——for he speaks of '*fo-*
'*reign countries*,' from which it 'would be
'*too far* to transport some kind of naval
'stores,' and for the same reason could *not*, he says, supply the sugars islands '*with*
'lumber and provisions.' He mentions also,
'planting colonies at *so vast a distance*, that
'the *very long transportation* (of silk, wine,
'*&c.*)

'*&c.*) muſt probably make them *too dear* 'for any market,' and *where* 'the inhabitants 'could *not* have *any commodities* to barter for 'manufactures, except *ſkins and furs.*' And what, in our opinion, fully evinces that the general was giving his ſentiments upon ſettlements at *Detroit*, &c., and *not* on the territory in queſtion, is, that he ſays, ' it will be ' a queſtion likewiſe, whether colonization of '· this kind *could be effected without an Indian* '*war, and fighting for every inch of the* '*ground.*' Why the Lords Commiſſioners for Trade and Plantations ſhould encumber their *Report* with the opinion of General Gage, on what he calls the ſettlement of a '*foreign country,*' that could not be effected without '*fighting for every inch of ground,*' and how their Lordſhips could apply that caſe to the ſettlement of a territory, purchaſed by his Majeſty near four years ago, and *now* inhabited by ſeveral thouſand Britiſh ſubjects, whom the Indians themſelves, living on the Northern ſide of the Ohio, (as ſhall be fully ſhewn in the courſe of theſe obſervations,) have earneſtly requeſted may be immediately governed,

governed, we confefs we are wholly at a lofs to comprehend.

"VIII. The eighth paragraph highly extols not only the *accuracy and precifion* of the foregoing Reprefentation of the Lords of Trade in 1768, (which, as has been before obferved, expreffed, that the inhabitants of the middle colonies *would have liberty to fettle over* the mountains, and on the Ohio,) but alfo the above mentioned letter from the commander in chief in America; and at the fame time introduces the fentiments of Mr. Wright, Governor of Georgia, ' on the fub-' ject of large grants in the interior parts of ' America.'

" When this letter was written, what was the occafion of the governor's writing it,—whether he was *then*, from his own knowledge, acquainted with the fituation of the country *over* the mountains,—with the difpofition of the inhabitants of the middle colonies,—with the capability of the Ohio country, from its foil, climate, or communication

nication with the river Powtomack, &c. to supply this kingdom with *silk, flax, hemp*, &c.—and whether the principal part of Mr. Wright's estate is on the *sea-coast* in *Georgia*,—are facts which we wish had been stated, that it might be known whether Governor Wright's ' knowledge and experience in the
' affairs of colonies ought, as the Lords of
' Trade mention, to give great weight to his
' opinion' on the present occasion.

" The doctrine insisted on by Governor Wright appears to us reducible to the following propositions:

" 1st. That if a *vast* territory be granted to any set of gentlemen who really mean to people it, and actually do so, *it must* draw and carry out a great number of people from *Great Britain*.

" 2d. That they will soon become a kind of separate and independent people, who will set up for themselves,—will *soon* have manufactures of their own,—will *neither* take supplies from the mother country, nor the provinces at *the back* of which they are settled. That being at such a distance from the seat of *government*, from *courts, magistrates,* &c. and *out* of the control of law and government, they will become a receptacle for offenders, *&c.*

" 3d. That the sea-coast should be *thick* settled with inhabitants, and be well cultivated and improved; *&c.*

" 4th. That his ideas are *not* chimerical; that he knows *something* of the situation and state of things in America; and, from some *little* occurrences that have happened, he can very easily *figure* to himself *what may,* and, in short, *what will* certainly happen, if not prevented in time.

" On these propositions we shall take the liberty of making a few observations.

" To the *first* we answer,—We shall, we are persuaded, satisfactorily prove, that in the middle colonies, *viz.* New Jersey, Pennsylvania, Maryland, and Virginia, there is hardly any

any *vacant land*, except such as is monopolized by great landholders, for the purpose of selling *at high prices*; that the poor people of these colonies, with large families of children, *cannot* pay these prices; and that several thousand families, for that reason, have *already* settled upon the Ohio; that we do not wish for, and shall not encourage one single family of his Majesty's *European subjects* to *settle* there (and this we have no objection to be prevented from doing); but shall *wholly* rely on the voluntary superflux of the inhabitants of the middle provinces for settling and cultivating the lands in question.

" On the *second*,—It is not, we presume, necessary for us to say more, than that all the conjectures and suppositions ' of being a ' kind of separate and independent people,' &c. entirely lose their force, on the proposition of a government being established on the grant applied for, as the Lords of Trade have themselves acknowledged.

" On the *third*,—We would only briefly remark, that we have fully answered this objection

jection in the latter part of our answer to the sixth paragraph.

"And as the *fourth* proposition is merely the Governor's declaration of his *knowledge* of *something* of the situation and state of things in America, and what, from some *little* occurrences, that have already really happened, he can very easily *figure* to himself what may and *will* certainly happen, if not prevented in time:—We say, that as the Governor has not mentioned what these *little* occurrences are, we cannot pretend to judge, whether what he *figures* to himself, is any ways relative to the object under consideration, or, indeed, what else it is relative to.

"But as the Lords Commissioners for Trade and Plantations have thought proper to insert in their *Report* the above-mentioned letters from General Gage and Governor Wright, it may not be improper for us to give the opinion of his Majesty's House of Burgesses of the dominion of Virginia on the *very point* in question, as conveyed to his Majesty in their address of the 4th of August 1767, and
delivered

delivered the latter end of that year to the Lords Commissioners for Trade and Plantations, by Mr. Montague, agent for the colony. The House of Burgesses say;—' We humbly
' hope, that we shall obtain your royal in-
' dulgence, *when we give it as our opinions,*
' that it will be *for your Majesty's service,*
' *and the interest of your American dominions*
' *in general, to continue the encouragements*'
(which were a *total exemption from any con-
sideration-money whatsoever, and a remission of
quit-rent for ten years, and of all kinds of taxes
for fifteen years*) ' for *settling those frontier*
' *lands.*' By this means the House observed,
' *New* settlements will be made *by people of*
' *property, obedient subjects to government*;
' but if the present restriction should con-
' tinue, we have the strongest reason to be-
' lieve, *that country will become the resort of*
' *fugitives and vagabonds, defiers of law and*
' *order, and who in time may form a body*
' *dangerous to the peace and civil government*
' *of this colony.*'

" We come now to the consideration of the 9th, 10th, and 11th paragraphs.

" In

" In the 9th, the Lords Commissioners for Trade and Plantations observe, ' That admitting the settlers over the mountains, and on the Ohio, to be as numerous as *report* states them to be,' (and which we shall, from undoubted testimony, prove to be not less than five thousand families, of at least six persons to a family, independent of some thousand families which are also settled *over* the mountains, within the limits of the province of Pennsylvania,) yet their Lordships say, ' it operates strongly in point of argument *against* what is proposed.' And their Lordships add, ' If the foregoing reasoning has any weight, it ought certainly to induce the Lords of the Committee of the Privy Council, to *advise* his Majesty to take every method *to* CHECK the progress of these settlements; and *not* to make such grants of the land as will have an immediate tendency to encourage them.'

" Having, we presume, clearly shewn that the country *southward* of the Great Kenhawa, quite to the Cherokee river, belonged to the Six Nations, and *not* to the Cherokees;—
that

that *now* it belongs to the King, in virtue of his Majesty's purchase from the Six Nations.; —that neither these tribes *nor* the Cherokees do hunt between the Great Kenbawa and the land opposite the Sioto River ;—that, by the present boundary line, the Lords Commissioners for Trade and Plantations would sacrifice to the *Cherokees* an extent of country of at least eight hundred miles in length, which his Majesty has bought and paid for;—that the real limits of Virginia do *not* extend westward beyond the Allegany mountains;—that since the purchase of the country from the Six Nations his Majesty has not annexed it, or any part of it, to the colony of Virginia; —that there are no settlements made under *legal titles*, on any part of the lands we have agreed for with the Lords Commissioners of the Treasury;—that in the year 1748, the strongest marks of royal encouragement were given to settle the country *over* the mountains ;—that the *suspension* of this encouragement by the proclamation of October 1763, was merely *temporary* until the lands were purchased from the natives ;—that the avidity to settle these lands was so great, that large settlements were made thereon *before they were purchased*;—that although the settlers were daily exposed to the cruelties of the savages, neither a military force, nor repeated proclamations could induce them to vacate these lands;—that the soil of the country *over* the mountains is excellent, and capable of easily producing *hemp, flax, silk, tobacco, iron, wine,* &c.;—that these articles can be cheaply conveyed to a seaport for exportation;—that the charge of carriage is so very small, it cannot possibly operate to the prevention of the use of British manufactures;—that the King's purchasing the lands from the Indians and fixing a *boundary line* with them, was for the very purpose of his subjects settling them;—and that the Commissioners for Trade and Plantations in 1768, declared, that the *inhabitants of the middle colonies* would have liberty for that purpose.—

" And to this train of facts let us add,— that the congress held with the Six Nations at Fort Stanwix in 1768, *when* his Majesty purchased the territory on the Ohio, Messrs. Penn also bought from these nations a very extensive tract of country *over* the Allegany mountains, and on that river *(joining* the very lands in question:—That in the spring 1769, Messrs. Penn opened their *land-office* in Pennsylvania for the *settling the country* which they had so bought at Fort Stanwix; and all such settlers as had seated themselves *over the mountains,* within the limits of Pennsylvania, *before* the lands were purchased from the natives, have *since* obtained titles for their plantations:—That in 1771, a petition was presented to the assembly of the province of Pennsylvania, praying that a *new* county may be made *over* these mountains:—That the legislature of that province, in consideration of the great number of families settled *there,* within the limits of that province, did that year enact a law for the *erection* of the lands *over the mountains into a* new county, by the name of *Bedford County*:—That in consequence of such law, William Thompson, Esq. was chosen to represent it in the General Assembly:—That a sheriff, coroner, justices of the peace, constables, and other civil officers, are appointed and do reside *over* the mountains:—That all the King's subjects, who are

not

not less than five thousand families, who have made locations and settlements on the lands *southward* of, and adjoining to the *southern* line of Pennsylvania, live *there* without any degree of order, law, or government:—That being in this lawless situation, continual quarrels prevail among them:—That they have already infringed the *boundary line*, killed several Indians, and encroached on the lands on the opposite side of the Ohio; and that disorders of the most dangerous nature with respect to the Indians, the *boundary-line*, and the *old colonies*, will soon take place among these settlers, if law and subordination are not immediately established among them. Can these facts be possibly perverted so as to operate either in point of argument or policy, *against* the proposition of governing the King's subjects on the lands in question?

" It ought to be considered also, that we have agreed to pay as much for a small *part* of the cession made at Fort Stanwix, as the *whole* cession cost the crown, and at the same time be at the entire expence of establishing and supporting the proposed new colony.

" The

" The truth is, the inhabitants settled on this tract of country are in so ungoverned and lawless a situation, that the very Indians themselves complain of it; so that, if they are *not* soon governed, an Indian war will be the inevitable consequence. This, we presume, is evident both from the correspondence of General Gage with the Earl of Hillsborough, and a speech of the chiefs of the *Delawares, Munsies*, and *Mohickons*, living on the Ohio, to the governors of Pennsylvania, Maryland, and Virginia, lately transmitted by the General to his Lordship.

" In this speech these nations observe, that since the sale of the lands to the King on the Ohio,—' *Great numbers more of your people*
' have come *over* the great mountains and
' settled throughout this country, and we are
' sorry to tell you, that several quarrels have
' happened between your people and ours,
' *in which people have been killed on both sides*,
' and that we now see the nations round us
' and your people *ready to embroil in a quar-*
' *rel*, which gives our nations great concern,
' as we, on *our* parts, want to live in friend-
' ship

' ſhip with you. As you have always told
' us *you have laws* to govern your people by,
' —but we do not ſee that you have; there-
' fore, brethren, *unleſs you can fall upon ſome*
' *method of governing your people, who live*
' *between the great mountains and the Ohio*
' *river, and who are very numerous,* it will
' be out of the Indians' power *to govern*
' their young men; for we aſſure you the
' black clouds begin to gather faſt in this
' country, and *'if ſomething is not ſoon done,*
' theſe clouds will deprive us of ſeeing the
' ſun. We deſire you to *give the greateſt at-*
' *tention* to what we now tell you; *as it comes*
' *from our hearts,* and a deſire we have to live
' in peace and friendſhip with our brethren
' the Engliſh, and therefore it grieves us 'to
' ſee ſome of the nations about us and your
' people *ready to ſtrike each other.* We find
' your people are very fond of our rich land;
' —we ſee them quarrelling with each other
' every day about land, and burning one
' another's houſes, ſo that we do not know
' how ſoon *they may come over the river Ohio,*
' and drive us from our villages; *nor do we*
' *ſee you, brothers, take any care to ſtop them.*'

" This

"This speech, from tribes of such great influence and weight upon the Ohio, conveys much useful information.—It establishes the fact of the settlers *over* the mountains being *very numerous*.—It shews the entire approbation of the Indians, in respect to a colony being established on the Ohio.—It pathetically complains of the King's subjects *not* being governed, and it confirms the assertion mentioned by the Lords Commissioners for Trade and Plantations in the eighth paragraph of their Report, ' That if the settlers are suffered
' to continue in the lawless state of anarchy
' and confusion, they will commit such
' abuses as cannot fail of involving us in
' quarrels and disputes with the Indians, *and*
' *thereby endanger the security of his Majesty's*
' *colonies.*'

"The Lords Commissioners for Trade and Plantations, however, pay no regard to all these circumstances, but content themselves with observing, ' We see nothing to hinder
' the government of Virginia from extend-
' ing the laws and constitution of that co-
' lony to *such persons as may have already*
' *settled*

'*settled there under legal titles.*' To this we *repeat*, that there are *no such* persons, as have settled *under legal titles*; and even admitting there were, as their Lordships say in the 10th paragraph, '*it appears to them*, there '*are some possessions* derived from grants made ' by the Governor and Council of Virgi- ' nia;' and allowing that the laws and constitution of Virginia *did*—as they unquestionably *do not*—extend to this territory, have the Lords Commissioners proposed any expedient for governing those many thousand families, who have *not* settled *under legal tiles*, but only agreeably to the ancient *usage of location?*— Certainly not.—But, on the contrary, their Lordships have recommended, that his Majesty should be advised to take every method *to check* the progress of their settlements;—and thereby leave them in their present lawless situation, at the risk of involving the middle colonies in a war with the natives, pregnant with a loss of commerce, and depopulation of their frontier counties.

" Having made these observations, it may next be proper to consider *how* the laws and
' consti-

constitution of Virginia can possibly be *extended*, so as effectually to operate on the territory in question? Is not Williamsburgh, the capital of Virginia, at least 400 miles from the settlements on the Ohio?—Do *not* the laws of Virginia require, that all persons guilty of capital crimes *shall* be tried *only* in Williamsburgh?——Is not the General Assembly held there?—Is not the Court of King's-Bench, or the superior Court of the dominion, kept there?—Has Virginia provided any fund for the support of the officers of these *distant* settlements, or for the transporting offenders, and paying the expence of witnesses travelling 800 miles, *(viz.* going and returning,) and during their stay at Williamsburgh?—And will not these settlers be exactly (for the reasons assigned) in the situation, described by Governor Wright in the very letter which the Commissioners for Trade and Plantations have so warmly recommended, viz. ' such persons as are set-
' tled at the *back* of the provinces, being at
' a *distance* from the *seat* of *government*,
' courts, magistrates, &c. they will be *out*
' of the *reach* and controul of law and go-
' vernment,

' vernment, and their settlement will be-
' come a receptacle, and kind of asylum for
' offenders?'

" On the 11th paragraph we apprehend it is not necessary to say much.—The reservatory clause proposed in our Memorial is what is usual in royal grants; and in the present case, the Lords of the Committee of the Privy Council, we hope, will be of opinion, it is quite sufficient, more especially as we are able to prove to their Lordships, that there are no ' possessions,' within the boundaries of the lands under consideration, which are held held ' *under legal titles.*'

" To conclude: As it has been demonstrated, that neither royal nor provincial proclamations,—nor the dread and horrors of a savage war,—were sufficient (even *before* the country was purchased from the Indians) to prevent the settlement of the lands *over* the mountains—can it be conceived, that, *now* the country is purchased, and the people have seen the proprietors of Pennsylvania, who are the hereditary supporters of *British policy* in
their

their own province, give every degree of encouragement to *settle* the lands *westward* of the mountains,—the legislature of the province, at the same time, effectually corroborate the measure, and several thousand families, in consequence thereof, settle in the *new county* of Bedford,—that the inhabitants of the Middle Colonies will *be restrained* from cultivating the luxuriant country of the Ohio, joining to the *southern* line of Pennsylvania? But, even admitting that it might formerly have been a question of some propriety, whether the country should be permitted to be settled;—that cannot surely become a subject of inquiry now, when it is an obvious and certain truth, *that at least thirty thousand British subjects are already settled there.*—Is it fit to leave such a body of people *lawless and ungoverned?*—will sound policy recommend this manner of colonizing and increasing the wealth, strength, and commerce of the empire? or will it not point out, that it is the indispensable duty of government to render *bad* subjects *useful* subjects; and for that purpose *immediately* to establish law and subordination among them, and thereby *early* con-

Vol. II. Y firm

firm *their* native attachment to the laws, traffic, and customs of this kingdom?

" On the whole, we presume that we have, both by facts and sound argument, shewn, that the opinion of the Lords Commissioners for Trade and Plantations on the object in question, is *not* well founded, and that, if their Lordships' opinion should be adopted, it would be attended with the most mischievous and dangerous consequences to the commerce, peace, and safety of his Majesty's colonies in America:

" We therefore hope, the expediency and utility of erecting the lands agreed for into a separate colony without delay, will be considered as a measure of the soundest policy, highly conducive to the peace and security of the old colonies, to the preservation of the *boundary line*, and to the commercial interests of the mother country."

In the year 1773, the House of Representatives of Massachusetts Bay sent to Dr. Franklin,

lin, who was their agent in London, a petition to the King, praying his Majefty to remove from their places, the Governor and Lieutenant Governor of the province [Thomas Hutchinfon and Andrew Oliver.]

This petition was founded on fome letters written by thofe gentlemen to Mr. Thomas Whately, who had been Secretary to the Treafury during Mr. Grenville's adminiftration. (See an account of them under the article of Mr. Whately, Chapter xix. Page 104 of this Volume.) The King having referred the petition to his Privy Council, to report upon it, they heard counfel upon it on the 29th of January 1774: Mr. Dunning and Mr. John Lee, for the petition, and Mr. Wedderburne, Solicitor General, againft it. Mr. Wedderburne's fpeech was an entire invective from beginning to end upon Dr. Franklin. The petition was difmiffed as groundlefs and vexatious.

Dr. Franklin told Mr. Lee afterwards, that he was not in the leaft hurt by Mr. Wedderburne's

burne's speech, but that he was indeed sincerely sorry to see the Lords of Council behave so indecently, manifesting, in the rudest manner, the great pleasure they received from the Solicitor's speech: that dernier court, he said, before whom all the colony affairs were tried, was not likely to act in a candid and impartial manner, upon any future American question. They shewed, he added, that the coarsest language can be grateful to the politest ears.

In answer to a bill in Chancery, filed against him on account of these letters, he declared upon oath, that he was ignorant of the party to whom they had been addressed; and that he had received them from a third person for the express purpose of conveying them to America.

His letter concerning the duel between Mr. Whately and Mr. Temple, the reader will find in the Appendix, in the article marked M.

He was immediately dismissed from his place of Post Master General in America.

When

When the American colonies declared themselves independent, the Congress restored him.

From this time the parliamentary proceedings against America, have been faithfully and fully related in the Parliamentary Debates, and Parliamentary Register. Finding that the British Ministers were resolved to break with America, he quitted England in the month of April 1775; and arrived in America in the succeeding month. On the day after he entered Philadelphia, he was elected by the legislature of Pennsylvania, a delegate to the Congress.

A few months previous to his leaving England, there was published a tract on American affairs, intitled, " An Appeal to the Justice and Interest of the People of Great Britain." It was printed from the manuscript of Mr. Arthur Lee, an American gentleman at that time in London, and brother to Mr. Alderman Lee, of the city of London. But Dr. Franklin had a considerable share in the composition; and it might now, with no impropriety, be called Dr. Franklin's farewell

well address. It was the most sensible and judicious tract on that side of the question. Many thousands of it were circulated.

In the year 1776, Lord Howe was sent to America to negotiate upon terms of reconciliation, and to continue the war, if the first did not succeed. The motives of the ministry in this measure, are amply explained in their speeches in parliament.

When Lord Howe arrived on the coast of America, he sent the following letter to Dr. Franklin; and received the following answer:

" Eagle, June 20th, 1776.
" I cannot, my worthy friend, permit the letters and parcels which I have sent you in the state I received them, to be landed, without adding a word upon the subject of the injurious extremities in which our unhappy disputes have engaged us.

" You will learn the nature of my mission from the official dispatches which I have recommended to be forwarded by the same conveyance,

veyance. Retaining all the earneftnefs I ever expreffed, to fee our differences accommodated, I fhall conceive, if I meet with the difpofition in the colonies which I was once taught to expect, the moft flattering hopes of proving ferviceable, in the objects of the King's paternal folicitude, by promoting the eftablifhment of lafting peace and union with the colonies. But if the deep-rooted prejudices of America, and the neceffity of preventing her trade from paffing into foreign channels, muft keep us ftill a divided people, I fhall, from every private, as well as public motive, moft heartily lament that it is not the moment wherein thofe great objects of my ambition are to be attained; and that I am to be longer deprived of an opportunity to affure you perfonally of the regard with which I am,

" Your fincere and faithful humble fervant,

" HOWE.

" P. S. I was difappointed of the opportunity I expected, for fending this letter at the time it was dated, and have been ever fince prevented, by calms and contrary winds, from getting here to inform General Howe of the commission with which I have the satisfaction to be charged, and, of his being joined in it.

"*Off Sandy Hook,* 12*th July.*

"Superscribed

"*To Benjamin Franklin, Esq. Philadelphia.*"

"Philadelphia, July 30, 1776.

" I received safe the letters your Lordship so kindly forwarded to me, and beg you to accept my thanks.

" The official dispatches to, which you refer me contain nothing more than what we had seen in the act of parliament, *viz.* Offers of pardon upon submission; which I was sorry to find, as it must give your Lordship pain to be sent so far on so hopeless a business.

" Directing pardons to be offered to the colonies who are the very parties injured, expresses indeed that opinion of our ignorance, baseness, and insensibility, which your uninformed and proud nation has long been pleased to to entertain of us; but it can have no other effect than that of increasing our resentments. It is impossible we should think of submission to a government that has, with the most wanton barbarity and cruelty, burnt our defenceless towns, in the midst of winter; excited the savages to massacre our peaceful farmers, and our slaves to murder their masters; and is even now bringing foreign mercenaries to deluge our settlements with blood. These atrocious injuries have extinguished every spark of affection for that parent country we once held so dear: but were it possible for us to forget and forgive them, it is not possible for you, I mean the British nation, to forgive the people you have so heavily injured: you can never confide again in those as fellow-subjects, and permit them to enjoy equal freedom, to whom, you know, you have given such just causes of lasting enmity; and this must impel you, were we again under your government, to endeavour the breaking our spirit by the severest tyranny, and obstructing, by every means in your power, our growing strength and prosperity.

" But

"But your Lordship mentions, 'the King's paternal folicitude for promoting the eftablishment of lafting peace and union with the colonies.' If by peace is here meant a peace to be entered into by diftinct ftates, now at war, and his Majefty has given your Lordfhip power to treat with us, of fuch a peace; I may venture to fay, though without authority, that I think a treaty for that purpofe not quite impracticable, before we enter into foreign alliances: but I am perfuaded you have no fuch powers. Your nation, though, by punifhing thofe American governors who have fomented the difcord, rebuilding our burnt towns, and repairing, as far as poffible, the mifchiefs done us, fhe might recover a great fhare of our regard, and the greateft fhare of our growing commerce, with all the advantages of that additional ftrength to be derived from a friendfhip with us; yet I know too well her abounding pride, and deficient wifdom, to believe fhe will ever take fuch falutary meafures. Her fondnefs for conqueft, as a warlike nation; her luft of dominion, as an ambitious one; and her thirft for a gainful monopoly, as a commercial one, (none of
them

them legitimate caufes of war) will all join to hide from her eyes every view of her true intereft, and will continually goad her on, in thefe ruinous, diftant expeditions, fo deftructive both of lives and of treafure, that they muft prove as pernicious to her in the end as the Croifades formerly were to moft of the nations in Europe.

" I have not vanity, my Lord, to think of intimidating, by thus predicting the effects of this war; for I know it will in England have the fate of all my former predictions, not to be believed, till the event fhall verify it.

" Long did I endeavour with unfeigned and unwearied zeal, to preferve from breaking, that fine and noble china vafe—the Britifh empire; for I know, that being once broken, the feparate parts could not retain even their fhares of the ftrength and value that exifted in the whole; and that a perfect re-union of thefe parts could fcarce ever be hoped for. Your Lordfhip may poffibly remember the tears of joy that wet my cheek, when at your good fifter's in London, you
once

once gave me expectations that a reconciliation might soon take place. I had the misfortune to find these expectations disappointed, and to be treated as the cause of the mischief I was labouring to prevent. My consolation under that groundless and malevolent treatment, was, that I retained the friendship of many wise and good men in that country, and among the rest, some share in the regard of Lord Howe.

" The well-founded esteem, and permit me to say, affection, which I shall always have for your Lordship, make it painful for me to see you engaged in conducting a war, the great ground of which, as described in your letter, is ' the necessity of preventing the ' American trade from passing into foreign ' channels.' To me it seems that neither the obtaining nor retaining any trade, how valuable soever, is an object for which men may justly spil each other's blood: that the true and sure means of extending and securing commerce, are the goodness and cheapness of commodities; and that the profits of no trade can ever be equal to the expence of compelling

compelling it, and holding it by fleets and armies. I confider this war againft us, therefore, as both unjuft and unwife; and I am perfuaded that cool and difpaffionate pofterity will condemn to infamy thofe who advifed it; and that even fuccefs will not fave from fome degree of difhonour thofe who have voluntarily engaged to conduct it.

" I know your great motive in coming hither was the hope of being inftrumental in a reconciliation; and believe, when you find that to be impoffible, on any terms given you to propofe, you will relinquifh fo odious a command, and return to a more honourable private ftation.

" With the greateft and moft fincere refpect, I have the honour to be, my Lord,
    " Your Lordfhip's
  " Moft obedient, humble fervant,
            " B. FRANKLIN.
    " Directed
" *To the Right Hon. Lord Vif. Howe.*"

On

On the 4th day of July 1776, the North American colonies, by their delegates in Congress, declared themselves to be " Free and Independent States." The several colonies now become sovereign states, immediately formed constitutions for their distinct governments. That of Pennsylvania was composed by Dr. Franklin, and is highly esteemed, as a fine system of legislation and jurisprudence.

The first step of the Congress, after the declaration of independence, was sending Mr. Silas Deane to France, to request permission of the French ministry, to purchase in France, arms and military stores for an army. From the reception that Deane met with, the Congress were convinced that France looked upon their cause with a very favourable eye: and upon this, they appointed Dr. Franklin their minister at Paris, with full power. A ship mounting thirty-six guns was equipped on purpose to carry him. He left Philadelphia on the 27th of October, and arrived at Nantz on the 13th of December 1776.

1776. The ſhip he ſailed in took two Engliſh veſſels in her voyage, and carried them into Nantz, where they were ſold for the benefit of the captors.

The public fact of Dr. Franklin's arrival in France, and the fact of the French miniſtry permitting theſe prizes to be ſold in a French port, were irrefragable and indiſputable proofs of hoſtility to Great Britain; and ought to have been conſidered and treated as ſuch. But the miniſters of Great Britain were afraid of a war with France; and France not being prepared for war, choſe to temporize. Dr. Franklin was honoured privately with all the countenance he could expect.

The Americans having at this time (April 1777) a conſiderable number of Britiſh ſoldiers and ſailors priſoners in their hands, Dr. Franklin applied by letter to Lord Stormont, the Britiſh miniſter at Paris, upon the ſubject of exchanging them for the like number of Americans, priſoners in England. Lord Stormont's anſwer was in the true ſpirit of of his Court; it was in thefe words, " The King's Ambaffador receives no applications from rebels, unlefs they come to implore his Majefty's mercy." In fix months afterwards, General Burgoyne and his whole army furrendered.

In the interim, between the time of making the application to Lord Stormont, and the furrender of General Burgoyne, Dr. Franklin's pointed electrical conductors at Buckingham-houfe were taken down; and Mr. Wilfon's blunted conductors were put up in their ftead. When the celebrated American Orrery was deftroyed by the troops under Sir William Howe, Dr. Franklin faid, " they ought not to make war on the fciences."

Two months after the furrender of General Burgoyne, the French entered into an alliance with the Americans, offenfive and defenfive. When this meafure had taken place, the Britifh miniftry made feveral attempts to open a negotiation with Dr. Franklin, but they
were

were too late. Mr. Pulteney, Mr. Conway, Mr. Hutton, and other gentlemen were sent to Paris for this purpose, but in vain.

Mr. Silas Deane and Dr. Bancroft, who was secretary to the American embassy at Paris, were accused of gambling in the English funds. Bancroft was dismissed: and though Dr. Franklin interposed in behalf of Deane, and made himself some enemies in America by it, yet he could not prevent Deane being recalled. This was very different from the conduct shewn to America, by persons in office, in London. The Congress dollars were forged in London, in immense quantities, and sent at different times to New York, Charlestown, and other places, with a view of depreciating and destroying the credit of the real dollars.

The attempt to negotiate with Lord Stormont, for an exchange of prisoners, having failed, towards the end of the year 1777 Dr.

gentleman, to London, with an application to Lord North upon the subject.

Mr. Thornton waited firſt upon Mr. Hartley, who, at Dr. Franklin's requeſt, attended Mr. Thornton to Lord North. This was on the 18th day of December, in the evening. Lord North received him very civilly. Mr. Thornton opened his buſineſs; but did not deliver a letter he was charged with from Dr. Franklin to Lord North. The converſation was nothing but ceremony, and an aſſurance to Mr. Thornton of perſonal ſafety.

On the 19th, in the morning, Mr. Thornton alone waited upon Lord North, and delivered to him Dr. Franklin's letter. Nothing but civility again; and a promiſe that he ſhould have an anſwer as ſoon as the other ſervants of the Crown could be conſulted.

Several days paſſed, and he received no anſwer. The miniſters differed with each other upon it. Lord Suffolk and Lord Mansfield were for maintaining the high anſwer given by Lord Stormont at Paris. Lord North and Lord George Germain were for an exchange of priſoners.

At length Mr. Thornton wrote to Lord North that it was a part of his inftructions to fee the prifoners, and therefore that he would go to Portfmouth and other places where they were confined, for that purpofe.

On the 30th, he returned to London: ftill no anfwer was ready. On the 2d day of January he fet out on his return to Paris. Next day an anfwer was fent to Mr. Hartley, ftating, that minifters intended, as opportunity fhall offer, to exchange them in America, againft Britifh prifoners there.

At the end of the month of March 1782, the Britifh miniftry were changed. In this change Mr. Fox was made Secretary of State for Foreign Affairs. Before he was warm in his feat, he gave a proof of his political fagacity, which none have exceeded—perhaps few have equalled. This was his open and manly communication to the Dutch. He took up the confideration of the war in Europe, upon a juft principle. He began with Holland, and thereby prevented a continental war. He immediately feparated the

Dutch from the Confederacy that had been formed against Great Britain. There was no longer any idea of joining the Dutch fleet to the combined fleet of France and Spain. The consequence of this disjunction was the relief of Gibraltar, which was closely besieged by the united forces of France and Spain. If the Dutch fleet had joined the combined fleet, which was intended, and there was nothing at that time to prevent it, Gibraltar could not have been relieved: with the addition of the Dutch navy against us, Gibraltar must have fallen. The British fleet at that time was not equal to the three maritime powers; Spain, France, and Holland. If Gibraltar had been taken, the conditions of peace must have been less honourable. The dates will shew the fact is indisputable. The resolution of the States General, " To request his Serene Highness, in his station of admiral-general of the Union, to concert in the most convenient manner with the court of France, a plan for the naval operations of the next campaign, so as to annoy the common enemy, in the most sensible manner," is dated on the 20th day of of February 1782. Mr. Fox was appointed Secretary of State on the 27th day of March following: and his letter to M. Simolin, containing his offers to the Dutch, is dated on the 29th day of that month; being the second day after he had been in office. This is as strong an instance of sagacity and penetration as will be found in the conduct of any former minister.

In the month of November following, Dr. Franklin signed at Paris the provisional articles of peace between Great Britain and America. And in the month of September 1783, he signed the definitive treaty, with Mr. Hartley.

He also negotiated, and signed, commercial treaties between Sweden and America, and between Prussia and America.

The tranquillity and independence of America being perfectly established, he requested to be recalled from the fatigues of his embassy; which was complied with.

Animal magnetism being a subject of much conversation in Paris at this time, the King appointed Commiſſioners to examine into the foundation of this pretended ſcience. Dr. Franklin was one of them. He preſently diſcovered the whole to be a mere trick; and as ſuch he reported it; which put an end to the impoſition.

In the month of September 1785, he arrived once more in America. He amuſed himſelf occaſionally with philoſophical reſearches, and experiments. It is not within the deſign of this work, to give an account of Dr. Franklin's philoſophical theories and ſyſtems. The reader will find them in his Works. This is a ſketch of the political part of his life, which is not in his works.

In the year 1787, a convention of the United States was aſſembled at Philadelphia. Dr. Franklin was appointed a delegate for the State of Pennſylvania. The purpoſe was to reviſe and amend the articles of Confederation, in order to give more ſtrength and energy to the government of the Union. He ſigned the new Conſtitution, and gave it his moſt hearty approbation.

In

In the fame year he eſtabliſhed two ſocieties at Philadelphia; one for alleviating the miſeries of public priſons, the other for promoting the abolition of the Slave Trade.

In the year 1788, his infirmities increaſing, which were of the calculous kind, he retired from all public buſineſs. During the laſt twelve months of his life, he was principally confined to his bed. He died on the 17th day of April 1790, at the age of 84 years and three months.

The following is a tranſlation from the *Journale de Phyſique*, for the month of June 1790.

" Franklin died in the month of April laſt, of an abſceſs in his breaſt. This great man preſerved his uſual preſence of mind almoſt to his laſt moments. Perſons public and private, of every rank and quality, attended his funeral, and probably there was never ſo great a concourſe in America on any occaſion. What an intereſting ſpectacle was this, of a whole people bewailing their benefactor!

The Congress, and various corporations, put on mourning for him during a month. The National Assembly of France, and a great number of other philanthropists, mourned for him three days. It is perhaps the first time that nations have mourned for a friend of humanity; whilst, to the disgrace of reason, we have seen them mourn for months together for its oppressors. All the nations of Europe are so submissive to the yoke, that they esteem it an honour and a duty to wear for several months mourning for one of their tyrants; whilst his death ought to be esteemed, and really is, a public felicity: such were the deaths of Louis the XIV. Louis the XV. Joseph II. &c. It is to be hoped that Philosophy will, in time, reform these abuses."

CHAPTER XXVI.

Messieurs BURKES.

Four of them. All Literary Men. Fugitive Papers. Series of Letters signed Valens. Answer to Lord Bath's Pamphlet. Answer to Dr. Franklin's Pamphlet. Importance of Guadaloupe. Lord Chatham of Mr. Burke's Opinion, but over-ruled. Value and Importance of the West-Indies. African Trade. Petition and Resolutions of the Yorkshire Committee. Mr. Burke's Letter on the Subject of them to the Buckinghamshire Committee. Several Particulars.

THERE were four of these gentlemen—The Right Honourable Edmund Burke; Mr. Richard Burke, his son, of whom nothing more need be said, than that he wrote an answer to an Essay or Letter written by Major Cartwright, which the reader will find in the Appendix near the end of the article marked

marked C; Mr. Richard Burke, brother to Mr. Edmund Burke, and Recorder of Bristol; Mr. William Burke, cousin to Mr. Edmund Burke, who was Secretary to General Conway while that gentleman was Secretary of State, and several years Pay-master in India.

The last mentioned gentleman has written several tracts; and it is more than probable, that he was frequently assisted by his cousin; and upon some occasions, there is no doubt, they were all three concerned; for they lived upon the terms of the most sincere friendship and affection. And although it is unquestionably true, that the talents of Mr. Edmund Burke had infinitely the ascendancy, yet those of Mr. Richard Burke, and of Mr. William Burke, were greatly above mediocrity.

An association of such literary abilities, and active minds, must undoubtedly have produced many papers, which are now unknown; particularly their occasional Essays, or Letters, in the newspapers; which they were in the habit of furnishing during several years.

years. Many of these are interesting, as containing the sense of parties, from the year 1764, or thereabouts. There were several in reply to the series of papers written by Mr. Scott of Cambridge, distinguished by the signature of Anti-Sejanus. If their friends have a correct knowledge of them, they would do well to collect them. There was a series of papers written by them, published in the London Evening Post, at the beginning of the American war, signed VALENS, from which some extracts have been made, which the reader will find in the Appendix, marked F, G, and O. They were ascribed principally to Mr. Richard Burke; but Mr. William Burke materially assisted, and Mr. Edmund Burke occasionally contributed.

When the late Earl of Bath published his pamphlet called " A Letter to Two Great Men," (Lord Chatham and the Duke of Newcastle,) upon the prospect of peace, in the year 1759, Mr. William Burke has always been said, and believed, to have been the Author of the answer to it, intitled " Remarks on the Letter to Two Great Men."

Men." Lord Bath having strongly recommended, in his pamphlet, the *retention* of Canada in the expected negotiations for peace; and asserted, that a preference should be given to Canada over Guadaloupe, or any conquests made in the West-Indies; Mr. Burke was of a contrary opinion, and argued strongly in favour of Guadaloupe.

Mr. Burke's pamphlet had sufficient merit to attract, and alarm the attention of Dr. Franklin; he therefore wrote an answer to it; which he intitled " The Interest of Great Britain considered, with regard to her Colonies, and the Acquisitions of Canada and Guadaloupe;" in which he coincided with, and enforced the opinion of Lord Bath.

Mr. Burke, though a young man, was not vanquished by his formidable opponent. He continued the contest by another pamphlet, which he intitled " An Examination of the Commercial Principles of the late Negotiation between Great Britain and France in 1761: in which the System of that Negotiation with regard to our Colonies and Commerce is considered."

sidered." This was published upon the failure of the negotiation between the late Lord Chatham and Mr. Buffy, in the year 1761.

As it is probable that Mr. Burke's argument may hereafter be useful, the reader will not be displeased with the following extract from it.

" The late negotiation, (he says,) so far as it regarded our colonies and commerce, was, on our side conducted, I apprehend, on one single idea, viz. to secure to ourselves the possession of all Canada. I say, upon this single idea, because from a careful examination of the several plans delivered to the French minister it appears, that even an attempt was not made, to procure in America any other possession, or any other advantage whatsoever. Our interest, and our conquests in the West-Indies, were very little, if at all, regarded. On the opening of the treaty we agreed to negotiate away Guadaloupe and Marigalante; and in the turns which that treaty took, and in all the different schemes of commutation, which were from time to time proposed, and they were many and various, I do not find that it was for a moment the idea to retain that acquisition we had made in the West-Indies, which the very article that restores it to France, denominates a fertile and wealthy island; [His Majesty likewise agrees to surrender to the most Christian King the *opulent* island of Guadaloupe, with that of Marigalante;] and which the very great increase of our trade since its reduction, demonstrates not to have been at all over-rated in those epithets, however it might be under-valued in the exchange by which it was to have been surrendered.

" The reader will not entertain any doubt, that the treaty was conducted on a principle wholly averse to West-Indian acquisition, when he recollects this remarkable fact.

" Early in the negotiation, and as I may say at the out-set, we agreed to exchange Guadaloupe for Minorca; but during the progress of that transaction, Belleisle fell into our hands. Here was presented a new subject

ject for exchange. It was quite natural to barter one European island for another; and it became the more natural, as one was of no great advantage to England, nor the other to France; and both were heavily expensive to their respective possessors. Accordingly, we find that exchange was proposed; but what is very singular, even at the time of making that proposal, it does not appear that any advantage was taken from this circumstance, to retain the least particle of our West-Indian conquests. The original scheme of compensation was changed; Belleisle was offered (so the French understood it) for Minorca; but Guadaloupe, the old equivalent, was, notwithstanding this new project, to have been surrendered; though not in exchange for Minorca, nor for any thing else that I can discover; and therefore, without any distinct compensation at all."

[Here the Editor begs leave to solicit the reader's permission to shew that Mr. Burke is in this point mistaken. We have Lord Chatham's own authority for the fact. In his speech in the House of Commons, when Mr. Pitt, on the 29th of November 1762, he he says, " He had been blamed for consenting to give up Guadaloupe. That cession had been a question in another place. (*The cabinet.*) He wished to have *kept* the island. He had been *over-ruled* in that point. He could not help it. He had been over-ruled many times, and upon many oc-occasions. He had acquiesced; he had submitted; but at length he saw, that all his measures, all his sentiments, were inimical to the views of those persons to whom his Majesty had given his confidence." No one will doubt, that Mr. Burke's arguments were well-founded. But as Lord Chatham was the negotiator, in the negotiation Mr. Burke is speaking of, it is necessary to accompany the passage in Mr. Burke's pamphlet, with this declaration of Lord Chatham; otherwise, Mr. Burke's statement would seem to impeach the rectitude and wisdom of that great Minister. But when Mr. Burke wrote his pamphlet, he could not be acquainted with the *real* fact; for it was not known, until Lord Chatham himself made it known.] We will continue the extract from Mr. Burke, because it is not uninteresting. The pamphlets of the day speak the sense of men in a

better

better manner than almoſt any future writer will take the trouble to repreſent them.

"Here alſo a difficulty occurs; for it is not eaſy to diſcover for what reaſon Belleiſle was taken, if it was not to be admitted among the equivalents. The expedition for the reduction of this iſland was undertaken after the commencement of the negotiation; and the place could ſcarcely be deſired for any other purpoſe than to give us ſome advantage in that negotiation; and yet a few days after we had taken Belleiſle, its negotionable value was eſtimated at nothing; and, in all appearance, we ſuffered it to be added to Guadaloupe, in compenſation for an object which had been before offered us for Guadaloupe alone.

"Had it indeed been neceſſary, by the ſurrender of the fertile iſland of Guadaloupe, to purchaſe the vaſt but unprofitable foreſts of Canada, the paſſion at leaſt of boundleſs empire would have been flattered. There had perhaps been ſomething magnificent in ſuch a deluſion. But from the beginning

Vol. II.   A a   there

there was no mention of an exchange of that nature. The first overtures to the treaty declare, that the privilege of the fishery at Newfoundland was the compensation for Canada."

[The words in the historical memorial of this negotiation are, " the liberty of fishing, and the shelter without fortifications, was the compensation for the cession of all Canada." The " restitution of the island of Minorca, was certainly equivalent to the cession of Guadaloupe and Marigalante." See the Historical Memorial, in the Appendix to the Anecdotes of Lord Chatham's Life.]

" The fundamental principle upon which all ideas of West Indian acquisition have been rejected, is a maxim laid down by the writer of the Letter to two Great Men, *that we had already sugar-land enough.*

" There is no word whatsoever of greater latitude in the construction, when it is referred to private concerns, than this word *enough*. With regard to the public, it is often contracted within very reasonable limits. Does it here mean that we have sugar-land sufficient to supply the home consumption? It is not strictly true, that we have enough for the consumption of all the British dominions. We know that in Ireland they use some, and in North America a very great quantity of foreign sugars, and syrups, and we have reason to believe that some find their way even into England. If he means that we have enough for foreign consumption, he is mistaken. Before the war we had almost lost the foreign market for this commodity. And unless he can prove that the sugar commerce is detrimental, I conceive this assertion equivalent to a declaration, that we have foreign trade enough. A declaration however repugnant to fact, and to the national interests, is altogether consistent with the system laid down in that letter."

Of the value and importance of the West Indies, Mr. Burke speaks thus:

" The direct import of Great Britain alone from the West Indies, in the year 1759, a year subject to the losses and casualties of war, and exclusive of Guadaloupe, which was then but just conquered, amounted to no less than 1,833,648 *l.* whereas the import from the great and populous northern colonies of New England, New York, and Pennsylvania, amounted but to 70,074 *l.* and the whole North American import together amounted to little more than a third of the West Indian.

" With regard to our dominions in Europe, there is scarce an article of British produce, which is not largely consumed in the West Indies. The benefit of the West Indian trade to our European dominions is not confined to Great Britain. Our island colonies, and they alone, take off a great quantity of provisions from Ireland; a consideration of no trivial consequence, not only from the connection of interest by which that trade binds together the several parts of our empire, but also because, whatever provisions go to our own colonies are so much taken from the markets of our dangerous rivals, and most determined enemies.

" Another

" Another confideration, and a very weighty one, is, that almoft the whole of that extenfive and lucrative trade which we carry on with the coaft of Africa, is maintained by, and muft be put to the account of the Weft Indies, becaufe the Weft India iflands form the great markets for negroe flaves.

" The trade to Africa is of the beft kind. It is for the greateft part fed with our own manufactures; our fire-arms, our ammunition, our utenfils, our ftuffs, and our fpirits; of all which we exported in the year 1761 to the value of 254,381 l. What remains of the affortment for that market, is compofed entirely of Eaft India goods, of which, in the fame year, it took off 78,576 l.

" Thus the Weft Indies fuftain, not only a large fhare of the direct Englifh trade, but alfo contribute very confiderably to the fupport of that mighty pillar of our national commerce and credit, the Eaft India Company. I muft beg leave to repeat it, and to fix it in the reader's memory, that the African trade centers in, and is fupported by the

West Indies; and that this trade, with its consequential advantages, is the principal dependence of the two, after London, the greatest and most flourishing trading places in Great Britain, Bristol, and Liverpool."

[Liverpool has now the principal share of the African trade.]

The calamities of the American war, and the acquiescence of Parliament in support of it, caused a general alarm throughout the nation towards the close of the year 1779. The extensive and very opulent county of York set an example of presenting petitions on public grievances, and of forming a general association, to give effect to the petitions. This example was followed by many of the counties and great towns in the kingdom.

Upon the subject of the Yorkshire meeting, Messieurs Burkes wrote a small tract, intitled, " The Yorkshire Question," &c. which the reader will find in the Appendix, marked R. It is not certain which of the Burkes is the author,—

author,—probably it is the production of the three.

The committee appointed at the Yorkshire meeting, agreed to a second petition in support of the first. A copy of the first petition the reader will find annexed to the " Yorkshire Question" in the Appendix. The following is a copy of the second petition; and of the resolutions which accompanied it.

" *To the Honourable the Commons of Great Britain, in Parliament assembled.*
" **The humble Petition of the Freeholders of the County of York,**
" Sheweth,
" That your Petitioners, sensible of the original excellency of the constitution of this country, most ardently wish to have it maintained upon the genuine principles on which it was founded.

" Your Petitioners further shew, That it is necessary to the welfare of the people, that the Commons' House of Parliament should have a common interest with the nation;

nation; and that in the present state of the representation of the people in Parliament, the House of Commons do not sufficiently speak the voice of the people.

" Your Petitioners therefore humbly pray this Honourable House to take into their most serious consideration, the present inadequate state of the representation of the people in Parliament, and to apply such remedy to this great and alarming evil, as to this Honourable House may seem meet.

" And your Petitioners shall ever pray, &c."

The several motions following were afterwards successively made and seconded; and the question being put upon each, it was

" Resolved unanimously, That this meeting having adopted a petition, requesting a reformation of Parliament in general terms, and being apprehensive, that from the generality of the petition, the intention of this meeting may be misconstrued, as aiming at a reformation of Parliament on principles and

to

to an extent which they do not mean to recommend, doth find it neceffary to declare that if,

" 1. A bill fhall be paffed in Parliament for abolifhing at leaft fifty of the moft obnoxious boroughs, providing for the electors in the feveral boroughs abolifhed a proper gratuitous compenfation for their extinguifhed franchifes; and enabling them to vote, together with other freeholders, in elections for knights of the refpective fhires to which they belong; and alfo adding an adequate number of members, not lefs than an hundred, in due proportion to the feveral counties and the metropolis:

" 2. And if the Septennial bill fhall be repealed:

" 3. And if a bill fhall be paffed for admitting proprietors of copyhold lands of inheritance, with fine certain, of the clear yearly value of forty fhillings, to vote at county elections of members of Parliament throughout the kingdom:

" 4. And

" 4. And laftly, if a bill fhall be paffed for fetting afide nominal and fictitious votes in Scotland, and for regulating elections to Parliament in that part of the kingdom, in a manner agreeable to the true intent and fpirit of the conftitution:

" The correction of parliamentary abufes, effected by thofe meafures, will eftablifh a reformation of Parliament which this county would highly approve.

" Refolved unanimoufly, That this meeting, trufting in the experienced zeal of their reprefentatives, Sir George Savile, and Henry Duncombe Efq. as far as circumftances will allow to promote the reafonable wifhes of their conftituents to accomplifh a fubftantial reformation of Parliament as aforefaid, and to fupport farther meafures of ftrict frugality, fo indifpenfably neceffary in the prefent condition of this country, doth poftpone offering to their worthy reprefentatives any inftructions on the faid matters."

This

This petition and these resolutions drew from Mr. Burke a strong letter upon the subject of them.

From Mr. Burke's pamphlet, called "Thoughts on the Cause of the present Discontents," it was known that he was hostile to a reformation of Parliament; but when some of the members of the committee of the county of Buckingham (being the county in which Mr. Burke resided) were known to have in contemplation an adoption of the conduct of the Yorkshire committee, and to recommend it to the second general meeting of the county, to be held in the month of May 1780; Mr. Burke wrote the following letter to a member of the committee; in which Mr. Burke states more explicitly than he has done any where else, his opinion upon the subject of Parliamentary reform.

(Copy.)

"Sir,

"Having yesterday heard, by mere accident, that there is an intention of laying before the county meeting, new matter which is not contained

contained in our petition, and the confideration of which had been deferred to a fitter time by a majority of our committee in London; permit me to take this method of submitting to you my reasons for thinking with our committee, that nothing ought to be haftily determined upon the fubject.

"Our petition arofe naturally from diftreffes which we *felt*; and the requefts which we made, were, in effect, nothing more than that fuch things fhould be done in Parliament, as it was evidently the duty of Parliament to do. But the affair which will be propofed to you by a perfon of rank and ability, (Earl Stanhope, then Lord Mahon,) is an alteration in the conftitution of Parliament itfelf. It is impoffible for you to have a fubject before you of more importance, and that requires a more cool and mature confideration; both on its own account, and for the credit of our fobriety of mind, who are to refolve upon it.

"The country will, in fome way or other, be called upon to declare it your opinion, that

that the House of Commons is not sufficiently numerous, and that the elections are not sufficiently frequent: that an hundred new knights of the shire ought to be added; and that we are to have a new election, once in three years for certain, and as much oftener as the King pleases. Such will be the state of things, if the propositions made shall take effect.

" All this may be proper; but as an honest man, I cannot possibly give my vote for it, until I have considered it more fully. I will not deny, that our constitution may have faults, and that those faults, when found, ought to be corrected. It is not every thing which appears at first view to be faulty, in such a very complicated plan as our constitution, that is to be determined to be so in reality. To enable us to correct the constitution, the whole constitution must be viewed together, and it must be compared with the actual state of the people, and the circumstances of the time. For that, which taken singly and by itself may appear to be wrong, when considered with relation to other things may

may be perfectly right, or at least such as ought to be patiently endured, as the means of preventing something that is much worse. So far with regard to what, at first view, may appear a *distemper* in the constitution. As to the *remedy* of that distemper, an equal caution ought to be used; because this latter consideration is not single and separate, no more than the former. There are many things in reformation, which would be proper to be done if other things can be done along with them, but which, if they cannot be so accompanied, ought not to be done at all. I therefore wish, when any new matter of this deep nature is proposed to me, to have the whole scheme distinctly in my view, and full time to consider of it. Please God I will walk with caution whenever I am not able clearly to see my way before me.

" I am now growing old; I have from my very early youth been conversant in reading and thinking upon the subjects of our laws and constitution, as well as upon those of other times and other countries. I have been for fifteen years a very laborious member

ber of Parliament, and in that time have had great opportunities of feeing with my own

vernment; of remarking where it went fmoothly, and did its bufinefs, and where it checked in its movements; or where it damaged its work. I have alfo had, and ufed the opportunities of converfing with men of the greateſt wifdom and fulleſt experience in thefe matters; and I do declare to you moſt folemnly, and moſt truly, that on the refult of all this reading, thinking, experience, and communication, I am not able to come to an immediate refolution in favour of a change in the ground-work of our conftitution; and in particular, that in the prefent ftate of the country, in the prefent ftate of our reprefentation, in the prefent ftate of our rights and modes of electing, in the prefent ftate of the feveral prevalent interefts, in the prefent ftate of the affairs and manners of this country, I am not able to vote that the addition of an hundred knights of the fhire, and the hurrying of election on election, will be things advantageous either to liberty or to good-government.

" This

" This is the prefent condition of my mind, and this is my apology for not going as faft as others may choofe to go in this bufinefs. I do not by any means reject the propofitions, much lefs do I condemn the gentlemen, who with equal good intentions, with much better abilities, and with infinitely greater perfonal weight and confideration than mine, are of opinion that this matter ought to be decided upon inftantly.

" I moft heartily wifh that the deliberate fenfe of the kingdom on this great fubject fhould be known. When it is known it muft be prevalent. It would be dreadful indeed if there were any power in the nation capable of refifting its unanimous defire, or even the defire of any very great and decided majority of the people. The people may be deceived in their choice of an object, but I can fcarcely conceive any choice they can make to be fo very mifchievous, as the exiftence of any human force capable of refifting it. It will certainly be the duty of every man in the fituation to which God has called him, to give his beft opinion and advice upon the matter;

matter; it will *not* be his duty (let him think what he will) to use any violent or fraudu-

or even of employing the *legal and constructive* organ of expressing the people's sense against the sense which they do *actually* entertain.

" In order that the real sense of the people should be known upon so great an affair as this, it is of absolute necessity, that *timely* notice should be given, that the matter should be prepared in *open* committees; from a choice into which *no class or description of men* is to be excluded, and the subsequent county meetings should be as *full*, and as well attended as possible. Without these precautions, the true sense of the people will ever be uncertain. Sure I am, that no precipitate resolution on a great change in the fundamental constitution of any country, can ever be called the real sense of the people.

" I trust it will not be taken amiss, if, as an inhabitant and freeholder of this county, one indeed among the moft inconfiderable, I affert my right of diffenting (as I do diffent fully and directly) from any refolution whatfoever, on the fubject of an alteration, in the reprefentation and election of the kingdom at this time. By preferving this right, and exercifing it with temper and moderation, I truft I cannot offend the noble propofer, for whom no man profeffes or feels more refpect and regard than I do. A concurrence, in *every thing which can be propofed*, can, in no fort, weaken the energy, or diftract the efforts of men of upright intentions upon *thofe points in which they are agreed.* Affemblies that are met with a refolution to be all of a mind, are affemblies that can have no opinion at all of their own. The firft propofer of any meafure muft be their mafter. I do not know that an amicable variety of fentiments, conducted with mutual refpect, and with mutual good will, has any fort of refemblance to difcord; or that it can give any advantage whatever to the enemies of our common caufe. On the contrary, a forced and fictitious agreement (which every univerfal agreement muft be) is not becoming the caufe of freedom.

freedom. If, however, any evil should arise from it (which I confess I do not foresee) I am happy that those who have brought forward new and arduous matter, when very great doubts, and some diversity of opinion must be foreknown, are of authority and weight enough to stand against the consequences.

" I humby lay these my sentiments before the county. They are not taken up to serve any interests of my own, or to be subservient to the interests of any man or set of men under heaven. I could wish to be able to attend our meeting, or that I had time to reason this matter more fully by letter; but I am detained here upon our business. What you have already put upon us, is as much as men can do. If we are prevented from going through it with any effect, I fear it will be in part owing, not more to the resistance of the enemies of our cause, than to our imposing on ourselves such tasks as no human faculties, employed as we are, can be equal to. Our worthy members have shewn distinguished ability and zeal in support of our petition.

petition. I am just going down to a bill brought in to frustrate a capital part of your desires. The minister is preparing to transfer the cognizance of the public accounts from those whom you and the constitution have chose to controul them, to unknown persons, creatures of his own. For so much he annihilates Parliament.

"I have the honour, &c. &c.
April 12, 1780.   "E. B."

The defence of Admiral Keppel on his trial is ascribed to Mr. Burke, in which he was probably assisted.

When Mr. Burke became Paymaster, in the year 1782, it has been lately stated, that he accepted that office with a view of reforming it. But his defence of Mr. Powell in the House of Commons does not corroborate that fact; and as to the reforming of the office, as far as that assertion has allusion to a prior Paymaster, the reader will find the authentic papers concerning it in the Appendix marked S.

Mr.

Mr. Burke's speeches at Bristol, not in his works, are also in the Appendix marked T.

It is not necessary to give an account of Mr. Burke's several publications; they will probably be printed in some future edition of his works; nor of his opinions concerning the American and French revolutions; which are to be found very fully detailed in his writings, and in his speeches in Parliament.

If ever Sir Henry Cavendish should publish his account of the debates in the British House of Commons, which he took in short hand, during the time he sat in it, which was from the year 1768 to 1774, Mr. Burke's speeches in that important period will appear with undoubted accuracy; and will give a more interesting picture of those times than any that has hitherto been exhibited.

END OF THE SECOND VOLUME.

University of California
SOUTHERN REGIONAL LIBRARY FACILITY
305 De Neve Drive - Parking Lot 17 • Box 951388
LOS ANGELES, CALIFORNIA 90095-1388

Return this material to the library from which it was borrowed.

val@library.uda.edu

5/23